Copyright © 2017 Foundr Media Pty Ltd

Disclaimer:
The advice provided in this publication is general advice only. It has been prepared without taking into account your objectives, financial situation or needs. Before acting on this advice you should consider the appropriateness of the advice, having regard to your own objectives, financial situation and needs. If any products are detailed on this publication, you should obtain a Product Disclosure Statement relating to the products and consider its contents before making any decisions.

Published by Foundr Media Pty Ltd
www.foundr.com

To contact the Editor:
Mail@foundr.com

Marketing opportunities:
Marketing@foundr.com

Cataloguing-in-Publication entry is available from the National Library of Australia.

ISBN: 9780995407008 (hardback)
9780995407015 (ebook)

Printed in Canada

Creative Direction & Design
JainKaran.com

Special thanks to:
Brian Bloom
Jill Greenberg
David Halliday
Aleks Witko

If I have seen further, it is by standing on the shoulders of giants.

Sir Isaac Newton

Introduction

For some budding entrepreneurs, making the decision to shrug off the 9-to-5 security blanket and start a business is not an easy one. For others—those among us who grew up fleecing the neighbors with our lawn-mowing services and lemonade stands— it's the only conceivable path.

The great news is, there has never been a better time to become an entrepreneur. The online economy has made the point of entry lower than ever, while a mix of social, cultural, technological, and market forces have combined to create unprecedented access to the global business playing field. It is, therefore, little wonder that we find ourselves in an era in which entrepreneurship and involvement in startups is at an all-time high. A 2015 report released by Global Entrepreneurship Monitor suggests that a whopping 27 million working-age Americans, almost 14 percent of the working population, are currently starting or running new businesses.

Like in any endeavor, there are risks associated with opportunity. But with today's business environment making it easier than ever to take the leap, it becomes harder to ignore the potential rewards of rolling up your sleeves and getting started. Few career paths allow you to be as creative, independent, or to exert such control over your own fate. And there's surely no other career that lets you shape your work habits to fit the lifestyle you want.

That's not to say the startup life is all beer and Skittles. In fact, if you're drawn to entrepreneurship because you see yourself drinking piña coladas in the Bahamas six months a year, you might think twice. As the contributors to this book will attest, it takes passion, commitment, and a healthy dose of hustle to make it to the top. But each of them is living proof it can be done.

And therein lies another reason it's such an amazing time to start a business—you don't have to do it alone. There is a sea of information out there waiting for aspiring entrepreneurs. When I started Foundr Magazine in 2013, my goal was to seek out and deliver the best of it to other people like me. To serve as a beacon, helping others navigate these vast waters.

Since our launch, we've interviewed some of the greatest entrepreneurs of our time, like Richard Branson, Arianna Huffington, Seth Godin, and Tim Ferriss, to name a few. But we haven't just interviewed them to talk about their success—we've gone deep, and broken down just what it has taken to get there and all of the lessons they have learned along the way. It's been such a ride, and we hope you've gotten as much out of it as we have.

The result to date, compiled here in *Foundr V1.0*, features advice and anecdotes gathered from our interviews with 50+ of the most impactful entrepreneurs on the planet. We harvested the best wisdom from our 130+ podcast episodes and close to 40+ magazine issues, and bound it all here in one entrepreneurial handbook. Collectively, these startup superstars have moved the needle for the rest of us in a major way, and influenced the way the world, and our society as a whole, operates.

Whatever stage of the game you're at, there's tremendous wisdom to glean from this cohort of rockstar entrepreneurs. Think of it as tales from the trenches, as told by those who have hacked, hustled, and harangued their way to the top.

Thanks for joining us on this journey. We hope this book helps you on yours.

nathan chan
CEO & Publisher
Foundr Magazine

chapter 01

GETTING
STARTED

01

FINDING YOUR PASSION

Everybody needs a reason to get out of bed in the morning, but this is especially true for the **unique group of rulebreakers and status quo-shakers we call entrepreneurs. It's us.** It's you. And it's that 8-year-old kid down the street who's been trying to sell you a used Christmas tree since January.

As entrepreneurs, without the driving force of our passion—the one pushing us forward and compelling us to work harder and longer than we think we are capable of—greatness would rarely be achieved. Problems would never be solved, nor creative solutions hacked.

Finding the thing that lights you up is, therefore, a huge piece of the entrepreneurial equation. If you're lucky, your passion is obvious—a deep-seated desire to solve a particular problem or effect a certain change in the world. For others, finding their inner spark calls for some trial and error, and for the rest of us, it's simply the idea of being an entrepreneur that gets the blood pumping.

Steve Blank is a startup-veteran-turned-author who is now using his experience to educate budding entrepreneurs. Widely touted as one of the "Godfathers of Silicon Valley," Blank has founded or contributed to eight startups, four of which have gone public, and now lectures at a number of high-profile business schools across the United States. Blank also helped to kickstart a little movement you might have heard of called the Lean Startup.

As Blank sees it, if you're the kind of person who has the passion to explore big ideas or to challenge the way things are done, you're already a cut above the rest.

"Founders, if you really think about what they're doing, they're creating something new that's never been done before. Who else does that? It's not accountants or clerks in a store—they execute a known set of things. The people who create great things out of nothing, out of just their vision, are sculptors, or painters, or writers, who look at a blank canvas and next thing you know, there's Starry Night, or see a blank score sheet and next thing you know, there's Beethoven's Ninth.

"Founders operate the same way. They have a vision of something that might be. Much like artists, it's that passion to bring that vision to fruition that drives you past all those miserable times. The good news is, we kind of understand that being an artist is a calling, not a job. The same is true for entrepreneurship."

steve blank

Tom Bilyeu is co-founder and president of Quest Nutrition—aka the second-fastest growing private company in North America, as recognized by *Inc. Magazine* in 2014—and he shared similar sentiments. In Bilyeu's experience, gained from building a company with a billion-dollar valuation within six years, pinpointing your passion is a matter of deciding what really matters to you.

tom
bilyeu

"It's not asking what opportunity can I exploit to make money, but what do I have enough passion to learn more about than anyone else in the world, and what will I fight my ass off for, even when it gets really hard. If you can align your business to that thing, man, you will be unstoppable. Human beings are so resourceful when they tap into their passion. It's just astonishing."

Bilyeu further identified passion as the reason he and his co-founders have rejected buyers willing to pay life-changing sums for their company. Being clear about their collective purpose—that is, not to sell a record number of protein bars, but to wipe metabolic disease off the face of the planet—has made it easy to turn their many suitors down.

"Money isn't our primary motivator—we just really wanted to go after one of the most major problems in society, and say, 'That's our problem to solve, we're going after that.' If you've got something you believe in that much, you'll stay hungry. But if you're just after the money, and you're thinking, 'What is the least I can do today to get what I want?' you will fade away."

While eradicating health problems is an admirable goal, many entrepreneurs getting started feel unnecessary pressure to pursue a passion that is similarly sweeping or earth-shattering. One of the greatest things about our current age of entrepreneurship is that whatever it is you love, there's a good chance you can track down an audience for it.

Just ask Michelle Phan, a YouTube icon who built an empire based on her online fashion and beauty videos. She started out in the very early days of vlogging, and her hobby has since grown into a global brand.

"You have to understand your audience before you create anything. You have to love what you're creating, and I always believe you need to be your own number one fan before anyone else. So create something that you yourself would love and enjoy and there's going to be a niche market that's going to love and enjoy what you love."

Of course, one problem familiar to so many entrepreneurs, especially those just getting started, is that they find themselves with too many passions. Some people are fortunate enough to have that singular mission that drives them day in and day out. But a lot of us are emotionally and intellectually pulled in many directions, which can make it difficult to pin down one business idea.

michelle phan

While business gurus typically recommend against trying to do too many things, Marie Forleo found that in her early career, finding her passion meant following her heart in multiple directions. A successful life coach, author, and motivational speaker, early on she found herself frustrated by the prospect of sticking with one corporate job, or even one entrepreneurial path.

"Every time I would read a career book or a business advice book, the last thing they would tell you to do was to do everything. It was all about focusing down, and it got to the point where it just became so painful for me. I thought, you know what, screw this. I cannot fit into any of these boxes. ... I gave myself permission to pursue dance and to start taking classes. I gave myself permission to do all the things I was actually interested in, and stopped trying to label myself as one thing. So I'd go to cocktail parties and people would ask me what do you do, and I'd say, which day of the week?"

Indulging her sense of wanderlust to pursue topics like dating, fitness, dance, and career coaching meant a crazy workload at times, but she also gained expertise in many areas. As her career evolved, Forleo was able to eventually focus in and synthesize work she loved most into one coherent business that she leads today.

01 GETTING STARTED

VISION

Once you have honed in on your passion, it's time to crystallize a vision. **What do you want to bring to life, and for whom?**

Many startup founders are intimidated by the idea of defining a formal vision, but it needn't be something you share with the entire world, or slap all over your marketing material. Rather, think of it as a way to keep your actions true and your business pointing in the right direction.

Former Elance CEO Fabio Rosati had a vision to change the way the global labor market worked. It was a lofty idea, but one that, remarkably, Rosati pulled off. The online services giant, which merged with oDesk before relaunching as Upwork in 2015, totally revolutionized the freelancing economy and is now used by more than 1 million companies, hiring from a pool of more than 12 million freelancers who collectively earn more than $1 billion annually.

Like most successful entrepreneurs, Rosati's journey has had plenty of twists and turns. Elance launched and went through several major overhauls before really taking off, a factor Rosati attributes to the company not having the right vision early on. Specifically, they weren't trying hard enough to revolutionize their space.

"I kept thinking about the vision, and not being in love with it. Despite being an interesting business, enterprise software wasn't going to change the world. This was when I realized that being in love with a vision is incredibly important, and so I convinced our investors to sell that business and we used some of the proceeds to fund a much more interesting version of Elance, which we launched in 2007."

Rosati further explained that to define a robust vision, founders should endeavor to strike a balance between purpose and innovation.

"People are increasingly motivated by purpose.

What's your purpose? What's your organization's purpose? Creating businesses today is a form of art, and the expression of that art. It starts with a vision of purpose. Successful businesses have a very crisp and clear vision that is well articulated and well understood by the people associated with that business."

fabio **rosati**

Leila

As the CEO and founder of Samasource, one of the largest social enterprises in the world, Leila Janah knows all about the importance of having a crystal-clear vision, especially when your mission is to create social good. Janah's goal was to tackle the problem of world poverty, not through charity, but by giving people the tools they need to move themselves out of poverty. Thanks to Janah, Samasource now employs more than 1,100 people, and has helped moved over 30,000 people out of poverty.

"I had this dream of starting a new model for digital work that would involve training really low-income people to do basic tasks on the internet so they could move out of poverty and companies could get their work done. This was the beginning of the outsourcing era, so we were just starting to see the rise of call centers and these types of big outsourcing operations, and I thought we could make this industry relevant for low-income people and use it to transform people's lives in very, very poor regions of the world."

leila janah

As important as it is to define that clear vision, others emphasize the need to stay nimble in what you're trying to accomplish. Businessman, author, and *Shark Tank* celebrity investor **Robert** **Herjavec** explained how, in the technology sector, an evolving vision is essential if you want to keep up.

"Every three years, I like to say, the tech space eats its own young. That's what happened to us. We found that the pace of change was something that took a long time to get used to. I think it's important to know where you are going, but, in tech, it can be difficult. So we have a short-term vision and a long-term goal, but we try to be focused on execution on a quarterly basis."

robert **herjavec**

However, Herjavec went on to say that when it comes to defining your big-picture vision, founders shouldn't be afraid to go all out. When explaining the growth of his principal business, IT security firm Herjavec Group, he told Foundr he wished he had set a bolder vision in the early days.

> "We're now a global company, we compete in the U.S., the U.K. I never imagined that we could do that. I grew up in Canada and all my businesses were in Canada, so our vision was to be the biggest company in Canada. Now, my vision is to be the biggest and the best player in my space, in the world, and I think, why can't I do that? It's just a level of confidence. I wish I had thought on a larger scale; it would have given me more growth, more incentive, and a greater vision to start with."

● ● ●

Being clear about these foundational attributes is also a great way to hitch people to your wagon, according to serial startup boss and Xero CEO Rod Drury. By selling people on your vision, Drury said, they can be confident they are working toward something bigger than themselves, which starts to propagate a culture of success.

> *"You have to lead by example, and set the values of how you're going to play. Create the charter your business will operate on, because there are so many decisions, you need to have a framework. What works really well at Xero—and why we have so many evangelists—is we have a really clear vision and we incrementally deliver to that vision. People get used to the flywheel of success as we keep having the courage to move in a direction, and executing on it. I'm always sharing and reinforcing where we're getting to, and just showing them that someone really owns the success of the business."*

Over the course of his accolade-rich career, AOL Co-founder Steve Case has also had a grand vision or two. Getting people's early buy-in on a little idea called the internet took more than a decade of perseverance. However, it was a failed merger between AOL and Time Warner that taught Case the importance of execution when it comes to delivering on a vision.

> *"The lesson I learned from that [merger] was that vision without execution is hallucination. The idea of the merger made sense to both AOL and Time Warner, but the execution was flawed. Ultimately, we didn't have the right people focused on the right priorities, or working together in the right kind of way. As a result, what could have been a transformative merger ended up struggling, and ultimately had to be unwound. The key lesson is, it really does come down to execution, and execution is about people."*

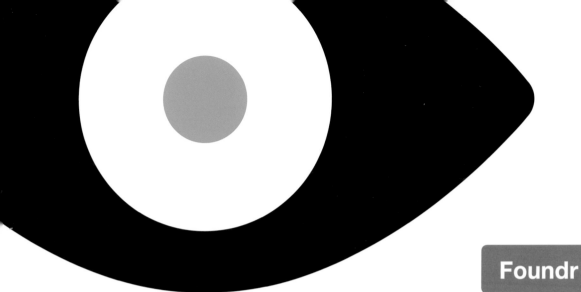

challenge your *own* vision

"Don't rest on your laurels. If you rest on your laurels, if you're not the one that innovates and even cannibalizes your own business, your own comfort zone, somebody else will."

**Fabio Rosati,
Former CEO, Elance**

As an entrepreneur, you're probably the type of person who tries to do seven things at once. While a can-do attitude is certainly a strength, it can become a point of weakness if your energies aren't focused on the right areas.

01 GETTING STARTED

GOAL SETTING

It's par for the course that you will wear many different hats, especially in the early days. But a consequence of spreading yourself too thin, or being too focused on the day-to-day minutiae, is that you can easily veer off course. Setting markers for yourself in the form of goals or milestones is an excellent way to stay on track. After all, if you don't know where the goal posts are, how can you aim for them?

Author and entrepreneur Chris Guillebeau set himself a goal and it became the catalyst for a successful international career. Guillebeau tasked himself with picking up a passport stamp for every country in the world by the time he turned 35. It was an epic adventure and one that led to the launch of his wildly popular blog The Art of Non-Conformity, and the *New York Times*-bestseller *The $100 Startup*.

Always intentional with his goal setting, Guillebeau takes time at the end of each year to do an annual review. He looks at what went well, what he was happy about, as well as his failures and struggles. Guillebeau then comes up with outcomes, and directs his energies towards them.

"A lot of people have **vague goals.** It helps to know what you really want and be willing to sacrifice for it, because you're willing to give something up in the short term to achieve something in the long term. **It's a universal** struggle. But what I do is I try to re-evaluate and regroup, and say: What am I working toward, what is this ultimately about, what do I really hope to achieve, and am I doing the right things to get there? If I disconnect somewhere, I need to address that."

chris **guillebeau**

Internationally renowned entrepreneurship expert Matthew Michalewicz concurred, believing the value lies in establishing goals for both yourself and your business. Having started several companies from scratch that later sold for tens of millions of dollars, Michalewicz has done the homework. He has also used his expertise to develop The Goal Pyramid, a handy tool that helps you visually unpack your goals, before breaking them down into milestones.

"Few people ever stop to think, 'How did I get where I am? Why am I doing what I'm doing?' Businesses regularly take stock, but most people fail to do the same. I advocate that people take time out. Stop. Think strategically about where you are heading and ask yourself, is that where I want to be going?"

matthew **michalewicz**

01 GETTING STARTED

THE LEAN STARTUP

The Lean Startup has been one of the hottest topics in the entrepreneurial world over the past decade. In a nutshell, lean methodology is a way to reduce startup failure rates and boost innovation, by speeding up the testing of ideas and the capture of user feedback.

Steve Blank's 2003 book, _The Four Steps to the Epiphany,_ is largely credited with launching the lean movement. Prior to its creation, Blank explained, entrepreneurs had been setting themselves up for failure by trying to execute fully formed business plans before their ideas had been proven.

"In the old days, you'd write a business plan—a document describing who you were, the opportunity, the size of the market, and you'd do a five-year forecast and if your VCs loved you, they funded you, and you simply executed against the plan. That is, you built the hardware or software, did alpha and beta testing and first customer shipment. Then you'd stand back and assume that the only thing you might have done wrong was whether the office was big enough to hold all the bags of money that were supposed to come in. And it almost never worked like that."

steve blank

Blank, together with a small group of industry thought leaders, devised a better way. What the Lean Startup aimed to address, Blank said, was the fundamentally flawed practice of trying to make startups emulate the behaviors of established, large-scale businesses.

"Startups, at least most of them, don't execute existing models. We typically don't know who our customers are, what our features are. All we really have on day one is a series of untested hypotheses. The word hypotheses means we're just guessing about all this stuff in a startup! So instead of executing a business model—here's the big idea—you're searching for one. And searching for one means, instead of just building stuff end to end, with every possible feature, you're in fact thinking, why don't I start talking to people outside my building, to actually turn those faith-based assumptions into facts, as rapidly as possible."

Blank goes on to define lean methodology as a series of steps, beginning with summarizing your hypotheses using Alexander Osterwalder's Business Model Canvas. The second stage, which Blank invented, is called Customer Development—a formal way of getting out and testing your hypotheses by talking to people. The third involves developing early prototypes.

"As you're going out talking to people, you're showing them a Minimum Viable Product, which is a fancy term for prototype. It might simply be a PowerPoint slide or a wireframe, or maybe some software, but it's whatever gets you the most learning at that time. If you use this process, you save an enormous amount of time and money, and you also save needing to fire a lot of people. Because, most of the time, you're going to discover that most of your hypotheses, your guesses about your business, were wrong. So you end up doing what's called a pivot. And a pivot says, let's make a substantial change to our hypotheses."

Martin Hosking, renowned CEO of online art giant Redbubble, is another Lean Startup advocate. He told Foundr that one of lean's main advantages is that it allows you to keep a laser focus on the customers. However, Hosking encouraged founders to ensure this single-minded customer approach is supported by a robust strategy.

"You need to have lean, but you also need to have a good strategic orientation. The customer doesn't always know what they want. So have absolute clarity about who your customer is. Have clarity on what your strategy is. Have a view about how you are going to make money. You do need to have an aspect of unrealistic passion to get there. But you need to factor in a view of what success looks like at any given point."

martin hosking

The Lean Startup: Steve Blank's Five-Minute Crash Course

Okay. We've heard about it. Everyone talks about it. But what is the Lean Startup? Foundr asked one of its pioneers, Steve Blank, and he gave us a concise rundown.

01

Business Model Canvas: Develop your hypotheses

"The first thing you're trying to understand as an entrepreneur is solving someone's problem or fulfilling someone's need." Exploring how your customers are solving the problem already, and why and how they would use your solution, is crucial to the process. This is where you put your hypotheses together. "This first step is about articulating and summarizing all your guesses about: Who's my customer? What are my features? Who's my distribution channel? How am I going to get, keep and grow customers? Pricing? Costs? Resources? Activities? The very first thing is to convince me that anybody else other than you cares about the problem and solution."

02

Customer Development: Test your hypotheses

Talk to potential customers, partners, regulators or anybody else involved in your potential business. As a rule of thumb, Blank recommends talking to a minimum of 100 people to validate your Business Model Canvas. "While you might spend two or three months doing this, in 90 days you've probably saved yourself a year-and-a-half worth of burn rates and frustration by actually learning all of this stuff, because people have taught you rather than you guessing!"

Put simply, it's a way to adapt business for the digital age to reduce startup failure rates and boost innovation. It speeds up the pace of testing new ideas, making use of the inexpensive and agile technologies of the internet and open-source software. It has three pieces:

03

Minimum Viable Product: Show your prototypes

The Lean Startup playbook teaches a rapid development of a Minimum Viable Product, designed with the smallest group of features to please a set of customers. Once shipped, the startup should continually experiment by tweaking its offering, noting how the market responds and altering the product accordingly. But the idea isn't that a Minimum Viable Product is a smaller version of the product. "It's whatever gets you the most learning at that time."

Foundr tips

STEVE BLANK'S TOP TWO MISTAKES TO AVOID

1. BELIEVING YOU ARE A VISIONARY
Almost every entrepreneur believes that they're visionaries. Data says about 98 percent of them are hallucinating. The distinction is that those who are actually true visionaries have got out of the building and tested their vision way before they spent a ton of money on it.

2. BELIEVING THE TECHNOLOGY IS THE COMPANY
The other mistake made by technologist entrepreneurs is believing that the technology is the entire company. Even if you have the world's greatest invention, your technology is going to die unless you figure out who the customers are, what the distribution channel is, what the pricing is, and how much it costs to acquire a customer. You need to figure out the rest of the commercialization components to the technology.

NETWORKING

Forging meaningful connections with a diverse range of people can have a profound effect on any entrepreneur's business. An important thing to remember, however, is the fact that networking is a two-way street, and should always be entered into with the right intentions.

Shaun Neff, founder of the eponymous snowboarding and streetwear brand, is one of the most down-to-earth founders you will come across. Neff is known for his laid-back approach, so it might surprise you to learn that he is also a master networker. He encouraged founders to show up at any event where there's a chance of making new connections, but also to accept that you won't know when, or if, any payoff will come.

"I'm a networking **freak**—that's kinda my game plan. But it's all about being real. A lot of businesses are pitched in a really sales-driven way, or the intent is not delivered as naturally as, 'Hey let's do something rad together and build on it.' From when I first started convincing pro athletes to wear my dollar headbands, I've just tried to be **real** and **authentic** and not give the impression that it's just about using their name on my brand to make money. I charter my evenings, my nights, around hunting down the right guys and just vibing out with them on a normal level. I always say if there is synergy, cool, and if not, here's my info and I'm sure our paths will connect later."

shaun neff

Productivity guru and *New York Times*-bestselling author of *Tools of Titans*, toolsoftitans.com, and *The Tim Ferriss Show* podcast agreed, describing how he spent his *4-Hour Workweek* launch budget flying to conferences and trying to grow his sphere of influence by getting to know relevant thought leaders. When meeting people under these circumstances, he kept a strict focus on having organic conversations, and only bringing up the book when asked about his work.

"I never pitched very hard, and I asked a lot of questions. I was very interested. I never tried to come in with a cape and show off everything that I knew. That is what created the snowball that turned into a massive monster—those one-on-one, in-person interactions that were not cold, hard sells. And 90-plus percent of those people I am still friends with. I identified exactly who was most interested and who was most receptive."

tim ferriss

jim
kwik

Leading brain performance coach **Jim Kwik,** who has trained the likes of Richard Branson, Jim Carrey, and Will Smith in the art of unleashing the mind's full potential, also reminds us that networking requires some basic human etiquette—like remembering people's names. As the founder of Kwik Learning and SuperheroYou, a global community of over 140,000 students, Kwik teaches a range of strategies for recalling important information. He believes the real reason people forget names when networking is because they simply don't take it seriously enough:

● ● ●

"People don't care how much you know until they know how much you care. So before you sell anything, whatever your business is, remember their name. I can't tell you how many people I know of who hurt a relationship or killed a deal because they forgot or said the wrong name."

jim kwik

Joel Gascoigne
Keeps Things Lean

■ Featured in
Issue 23 -
*Consistently
Happy: Behind
the Scenes at
Buffer*

Founder
Joel Gascoigne

Job
**CEO and Co-founder
of Buffer**

Success Story
**Buffer went from an idea to a product with
paying customers in just seven weeks,
and went on to hit 1 million users.**

A core concept of the Lean Startup methodology is the
idea of the Minimum Viable Product, or MVP. This is the
bare bones of your product idea, basically a prototype or a
beta. But it can be even more bare bones than you might
expect.

The point of creating an MVP is that, instead of wasting
resources building out a product that no one wants,
you can instead incorporate your customer into your
development process by going to market with your MVP
first. By doing so, you can validate your idea and see if
there's even a market for what you're creating in the
first place.

At this stage, you're really only looking for market
validation, so the substance of what you're offering can be
very light.

Just take a look at how Joel Gascoigne went from an
idea to paying customers in just seven weeks with his own
startup Buffer. A huge advocate for going lean, Gascoigne
started with the idea to create an easy-to-use app that
allowed you to schedule posts on Twitter without having
to manually set a time for each individual tweet.

▼

So how did he apply the Lean Startup methodology to his idea?

As it turns out, the MVP for what would eventually be known as Buffer wasn't even a product at all. Before he even began coding, all Gascoigne did was create a simple landing page that advertised the feature of his tool, a pricing plan page, and a signup link. After that, he just tweeted out a link to his landing page and waited to see if anyone would respond.

That's right—before he even began to build a working prototype of his product, Gascoigne started marketing it. In accordance with the Lean Startup methodology, the goal was simple: to see if anyone would be interested.

After receiving several responses, he knew that he had successfully validated his idea and had a viable product on his hands.

From there, it was just a matter of building the first working version of Buffer that was "good enough" to go to market. No bells or whistles, just a plain app that performed as advertised.

But the journey didn't end there.

A core part of lean is continuous development and learning. Just because his initial app was proving to be successful did not mean that Buffer was complete, far from it.

While Gascoigne had proven that he had a solid idea, it was time to let the idea evolve as organically as possible, something that's only achievable by listening to your users.

After gathering feedback from their early adopters, the team at Buffer realized there was a variety of features that their customers wanted. Not long after, people could use Buffer to automatically schedule their posts across multiple social media platforms, not just Twitter.

After that first iteration, they listened to their customers again and began working on the next version of their product. This time, a simple plugin for web browsers made it even easier for customers to schedule their posts.

By focusing on their customer first and foremost, Buffer wasted no time or resources on developing features or even an entire product that nobody wanted. Within seven weeks, Buffer went from a basic idea to a product with paying customers. It was plain and simple, but that's all it needed to be in order to get started.

Tim Ferriss is Just a Guy (Who Wrote a Book) Making Friends

Featured in Issue 27 - Hacking Time: How Tim Ferriss Turned His Quest for Productivity Into a Way of Life for a Generation of Entrepreneurs

Founder
Tim Ferriss

● ● ●

Job
***New York Times*-bestselling author and angel investor**

Success Story
With his groundbreaking book *The 4-Hour Workweek,* Ferriss inspired an army of entrepreneurs, and followed it up with a series of smash hits and a successful investing career.

Networking is super important for any entrepreneur, regardless of your level of experience, or what niche you're in. Having a strong network can open up multiple doors for you, whether that means helping you build other connections, or opportunities to further your career.

Case in point, Tim Ferriss can trace much of his success back to one networking event in 2007.

Today, Ferriss is a bestselling author multiple times over, with his highly influential book *The 4-Hour Workweek* topping the *New York Times* and *Wall Street Journal* bestseller lists.

That book established Ferriss as one of the most influential

people of his generation, inspiring countless others to start their own businesses, or at least change the way they manage their time. Since then, he's written two other bestselling books, starred in his own TV show, launched a highly popular podcast, and became an angel investor and adviser to many successful startups.

Back in 2007 though, Ferriss was an unknown. He had founded a moderately successful nutritional supplement company, but he was far from influential. In fact, he had taken his first, signature book to 25 different publishers and was rejected by every single one before being accepted by the 26th.

▼

Ferriss knew that it wasn't enough to produce a great book. If he wanted it to be a success, he had to get it into the hands of the right people.

It wasn't enough to contact people by phone or pitch his book by email. Instead, he realized he'd make a much stronger impact if he spoke to them in person and established an actual relationship.

"I spent my [book] launch budget flying to conferences and trying to spend time with thought leaders over coffee in the hallway or in bars. I bought a lot of drinks for a lot of people," Ferriss says.

In 2007, Ferriss found himself at the South by Southwest conference in Austin, Texas. In the lounges where they served drinks, Ferriss struck up a conversation with any influencer he thought might be interested in his book.

While the ultimate goal was to make people aware of his book, Ferriss's aim was to develop a real, organic relationship with everyone he spoke with, only bringing up the book when the conversation called for it.

By the end of the endeavor, almost every individual he had a conversation with didn't feel like they were being pitched to, or that they were given a hard sell. Instead, they were legitimately curious and interested in this book their new friend had just published.

"That is what created the snowball that turned into a massive monster— those one-on-one personal interactions that were not cold, hard sells. And 90-plus percent of those people I am still friends with. I identified exactly who was most interested and who was most receptive."

At the end of the conference, Ferriss had successfully networked and formed friendships with his target audience. The result was that multiple influencers found themselves reading *The 4-Hour Workweek* and were hooked. Word-of-mouth quickly spread and Ferriss found himself at the head of a cultural movement.

While Ferriss's meteoric rise might look like an overnight success to the untrained eye, it was carefully constructed through hours upon hours of sincere networking and forming the right connections with the right people.

chapter 02
PRODUCT

FOCUS

According to entrepreneur **Justin Kan**—who co-founded hit companies Justin.tv, Socialcam, Exec and Twitch, which he sold to Amazon for a cool $970 million—lack of focus is the single biggest obstacle for early-stage founders. "Issues happen when people don't focus on just one thing. They build something that never has product-market fit."

When it comes to
deciding which
of your ideas
to focus on,
business magnate
Richard Branson
told Foundr
there's no clear
formula. Instead,
he encouraged
founders to
balance facts with
the all-important
gut feeling.

"I definitely go on gut instinct, but it has always had the backup of research and information. Never be frightened of taking risks, and always follow your instincts! Don't be afraid to take that leap into the unknown."

richard branson

Melanie **Perkins**, whose design website *Canva* has been a runaway success, securing 8 million users in just two years, shared similar sentiments, believing a well-defined product focus is tantamount to success.

"The most important thing at the start is to make sure you really believe in what you are trying to achieve, and you are solving a problem that is worth solving. You want to get that fundamental thing so right."

melanieperkins

Having spent 10 years mentoring aspiring entrepreneurs, **Jessica** Livingston, co-founder of startup institution Y Combinator (YC), also offered up a ton of product-centric advice to Foundr. In Livingston's experience, two things help founders define their product focus: knowing the problem you are trying to solve, and starting a business based on an area of experience. In illustrating her point, Livingston told the story of Airbnb founders and YC alumni Joe Gebbia, Brian Chesky, and Nathan Blecharczyk.

"A lot of people don't realize how humble Airbnb's beginnings were and how often they were rejected. But also how focused their idea was when they got started, which is so important for aspiring entrepreneurs to take note of. You don't start building the grand idea, you start in an extremely focused and narrow way and you go from there. These guys started out renting air mattresses in their apartment during conferences."

jessica
Livingston

Robin Chase, co-founder and former CEO of Zipcar, one of the world's largest car-sharing services, similarly encouraged founders to solve problems they have direct experience with. Personal life experience can make an individual the exact right person to be doing certain things, she said.

"Instead of trying to be someone you're not, or starting with things that are very far from you, think about problems that are within your life, that you see and are irritated by, and try to solve those."

But even if you have a great premise, as it turned out Chase and her partners did, you can still very easily lose focus and go overboard early on in the process. She shared her experience of launching an early version of Zipcar, which resulted in a three-month delay thanks to a website that convoluted what they were trying to do at the time.

"I spent a lot of money building this website and it was way, way, way too clever, so by the time it hit consumers, I had overbuilt it. So we spent the first three months un-building it. When you think about the smallest thing you can do to start your company—whatever you think that is—it's smaller. Even smaller than what you think is the least you have to do."

Simplicity was also at the heart of Kenneth "Hap" Klopp's advice for getting started. After taking over The North Face from its original founders in 1968, Klopp spent the next two decades building the brand into a household name in outdoor recreation. In Klopp's experience, even the most straightforward businesses tend to have too much going on, despite the fact that a more focused product is easier to sell:

"More isn't better; more is harder to execute. Execution comes from simplicity; the essence is easy to execute."

"Stick to an area in which you have a deep knowledge, and can understand the nuances around what is broken and how any current solutions might be improved upon."

Jessica Livingston
Founding Partner,
Y Combinator

02 PRODUCT

UNIQUE SELLING PROPOSITION

Standing out has never been quite so important as in today's noisy, digitally driven marketplace, where a relentless stream of messages vie for our attention. Nailing your product or service's unique selling proposition (USP) can therefore be the difference between getting lost in a sea of voices, and hitting potential customers right between the eyes.

Defining a robust USP requires founders to do more than simply create a roll call of features and benefits. It's a matter of connecting your product or service to potential customers in a meaningful way, and amplifying all of its truly original qualities.

IF THERE'S ONE MAN WHO UNDERSTANDS THE IMPORTANCE OF LOCKING DOWN A PRODUCT OR SERVICE'S USP, IT'S RICHARD BRANSON. AS THE POSTER BOY FOR SEVERAL GENERATIONS OF AMBITIOUS BUSINESS HOPEFULS, BRANSON HAS LAUNCHED DOZENS OF GAME-CHANGING PRODUCTS, AND A FEW DUDS, AS EVEN THE MAN HIMSELF ADMITS. BRANSON BELIEVES NAILING YOUR USP IS SIMPLY A MATTER OF HOW WELL YOU UNDERSTAND YOUR AUDIENCE.

"First and foremost, a successful business must have a sound knowledge of its market, and work on how its product or service will be different, stand out, and improve people's lives," Branson said. *"If you can ensure it responds to a real need out there in the marketplace, your business can punch well above its weight."*

Establishing what your customers need up front is also a foundational element of the Lean Startup approach propagated by entrepreneur-turned-educator Steve Blank. He encouraged founders to start with the problem or need and then tease out their product hypothesis by asking a few key questions.

According to Blank: "The first thing you're trying to understand as an entrepreneur is solving someone's problem or fulfilling someone's need. This first step is about articulating and summarizing all your guesses about: Who's my customer? What are my features? Who's my distribution channel? How am I going to get, keep, and grow customers? Pricing? Costs? Resources? Activities? The very first thing is to convince me that anybody else other than you cares about the problem and solution."

Daymond John is another career entrepreneur and investor who sees a constant stream of product ideas through his role on *Shark Tank*. When it comes to nailing your USP, John believes it's about creating something that jumps out at people, so they will clamor to get their hands on it—much like they did with his game-changing streetwear line FUBU in the 1990s.

"You've got to come up with something distinctive. Instead of it being a 'me too' product, make it an 'I have to have' product. Then, make sure it's quality and that people have a strong connection to it."

DAYMOND JOHN

GRETTA

ROSE

VAN

Australian-born entrepreneur Gretta Rose van Riel built her suite of products in a very different climate than when John got his start, but a similar strategy has helped to explode each of her brands. As the creator of SkinnyMe Tea, The Fifth Watches, Nichify, and DROP Bottle, van Riel has found launching a successful product is a matter of identifying an emerging market and coming up with a better offer than what is currently available—jumping into the lead with a must-have.

RIEL

UNIQUE SELLING PROPOSITION

In the case of van Riel's watch brand, The Fifth, she also came up with a clever marketing tactic that gave the product a boost of excitement and demand. By offering a limited range of timepieces on the fifth day of each month for five days at a time, she's created a powerful, rolling demand that has delivered exceptional results—The Fifth pulled in $1.2 million in one month, just six months post-launch.

● ● ●

"With my product businesses, I've found it most helpful to look at a successful trending product, and then change one element or one dimension of that product. It's about making a product better, and then utilizing your audience. With The Fifth, we also use a mixture of inclusivity and exclusivity in our marketing. Rather than just selling a timepiece, we limited the time they were available, so they became a bit more exclusive."

Gretta Rose van Riel

02 PRODUCT
PROTOTYPING

steve

blank

Before you jump into full-scale development, prototyping is another vital early step in the lifecycle of your product. Prototyping gives you a tangible jumping off point, one you can feel and touch, and it allows you to interrogate important aspects like design and functionality, as well as the production process itself.

In his books, Lean Startup guru Steve Blank teaches a three-phase Customer Development Model, of which early prototyping is a key component. Blank suggests that, as a rule of thumb, you show your prototype to 100 people within a condensed timeframe, to validate your Business Model Canvas. Then, use agile engineering to build a Minimum Viable Product.

"This is a formal way of simply getting out of your building and testing those hypotheses. Talking to potential customers or partners or regulators or anybody else who is involved in your potential business. While you might spend two or three months doing this, in 90 days you've probably saved yourself a year and a half worth of burn rates and frustration by actually learning all of this stuff, because people have taught you rather than you guessing."

Blank further explained that this fact-based information will go a long way toward convincing investors of your product's viability:

"We learned something over 30 years of innovation in Silicon Valley and that was— no business plan survives first contact with customers. And let me tell you, the difference between a plan that actually is fact-based versus one that is faith-based, really might make the difference with investors."

Case in point is **Ankur Nagpal's** landmark online learning platform Teachable, which burst onto the scene as Fedora in 2013, just as the online world was seeing a major spike in the demand for quality digital courses. Nagpal also told Foundr how a basic prototype helped him get early traction with Silicon Valley investors when he went to raise seed funding.

"I'm the worst developer in the world. Ask anybody at Teachable and they will tell you! But I knew enough to build what I wanted. All it could really do was validate an idea, but that was all I needed. My biggest mistake was that I waited too long to consider the idea validated. We raised money six or seven months after launching, when it could have been two or three. I think it was my own fear holding me back. In retrospect, I should have seen the signs earlier."

● ● ● **ankur** nagpal

EARLY ADOPTERS

If there is one vital step in the early product phase that almost every Foundr interviewee has mentioned, it's the power of speaking to early adopters—that first, often modest, community of people who put their hands up to request your product or service.

Xero's **Rod Drury** discovered the significant role this early audience can play in your future success, with some of his early adopters valuing those interactions enough to take on integral roles in the development of the company.

"

With such little functionality back in the early days, looking back, it's amazing we managed to get off the ground. But we did and we learned a lot and we tried to give those early customers a really good experience. And they felt like they were part of a journey. Many even became shareholders and have done really well."

rod
drury

It's a similar tale to the one told by Eventbrite founding duo Kevin and Julia Hartz. From the outset, the pair's paradigm-shifting ticketing platform, since valued at $1 billion, has benefited from receiving intimate feedback from a small, but vocal, group of early adopters, said Julia Hartz:

"We felt that if we could get an early adopter group to start using the product, that word-of-mouth, and sort of virtuous cycle of people attending events and discovering the product that way, would have some impact on our business. We were proactive in finding an early adopter group in tech bloggers who were hosting meetups. We actively on-boarded them and not only were they active users, but they were also vocal in what they needed, and they helped us shape the product."

kevin & **julia hartz**

Go to the Source

"You want to get as close to a customer as fast as you can, so you can learn from **real people,** not what is going on in **your mind.**"

Robin Chase
Zipcar Co-founder

02 PRODUCT
Iteration

Once that early customer feedback is in hand, ongoing product development is what attracts new customers, and keeps the company relevant to existing ones. We call this iteration—the constant tinkering and fine-tuning to build a good spark of a concept into something truly great.

Drift CEO David Cancel goes so far as to suggest founders assume every idea they have is wrong. In his view, such a mindset makes it possible to get out there and test, so you can work out where your weak points lie.

"Never stop
improving on
your products.
The first version
is never the final
version—it is
a game of
iteration."

DAVID CANCEL

In a similar vein, in
her time at the helm of
Y Combinator, Jessica
Livingston has watched as
many successful startups began
one way before evolving in
a completely new direction.
They often retain a kernel of
the original idea, she says,
but will end up in a very
different place. "If you get too
attached to a certain direction,
you're probably going to fail.
Reinvention is part of
the process."

This was certainly the case for Buffer Co-founder and CEO **Joel Gascoigne**, who used a past experience with building a failed product as a reminder to himself to stay agile while developing the popular social media tool.

"When I started building Buffer, I had already experienced building a previous product where things did not go quite according to plan. Luckily, this prepared me to be patient with uptake of the service, and to be willing to change things quite a lot until I reached something that would be truly valuable for people. It also taught me the value of customer development: to take advantage of those emails coming in by asking people questions."

JOEL GASCOIGNE

Iteration doesn't always mean overhauling your product or scrapping original plans, however. For Teachable's Ankur Nagpal, iteration is a matter of doubling down on the things you do well, instead of bending over backward to implement every piece of functionality that is requested. Some companies spend too much time apologizing for what their product doesn't do, instead of focusing on what they offer.

"The highest leverage point we can have is building the most amazing product in the world. There are certain things people like and there are weaknesses, like a perceived lack of certain functionality. But **we have two** choices. We can either compensate for the missing features, **or we can double down on our** strengths. People think we make their sites look beautiful; I want it to be more beautiful."

Whatever people think you are good at, do that better, and then worry about people who aren't happy.

ankur **nagpal**

EMBRACE CHANGE.

02 PRODUCT

WHEN TO SHIP

Once you have a viable product, **the next big question** **is when to release it en masse.** It can be a difficult decision, one that cult tech startup figure and author Guy Kawasaki—the man famed for spearheading Apple's marketing in the 1980s before leading a number of high profile startups—believes is rarely straightforward. Kawasaki does, however, suggest most companies wait too long.

"You can ship something that is viable and can make a buck, but it is not necessarily valuable in the sense that it changes the world. You don't always know when to ship, but companies usually ship too late rather than too early. One good test is when you're about to run out of money!"

guy

kawasaki

start

SMALL

SETH GODIN

Fellow marketing icon **Seth Godin** agrees. The founder of Squidoo.com, and world-renowned author of 17 business bestsellers, believes the go-big-or-go-home mentality propagated by some startup circles can lead to paralysis, and a delay in planting the necessary seeds for growth.

sethgodin

"Start small, and start now. Start shipping a small amount of work and start putting ideas into the world. Watch them morph and grow and change people," Godin says. That could even mean shipping something people will pay you just $5 for. "Put an idea into the world that someone will respond to. Aim to create something that will delight your customer."

Of course, for all this inspiring encouragement to launch fast and get your ideas into the world, *Shark Tank*'s Daymond John grounded us with the reminder that you still have to be able to deliver on customer expectations, once you have shown them something they want.

"Find vehicles to distribute, and make sure people can get it after they see it. Don't go and launch an entire line of 50 things you can't put in people's hands—you will frustrate them if they try to get a hold of something and can't find it. You've got to fulfil the consumer's request."

Forget

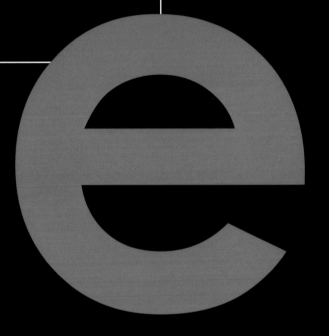

P

er

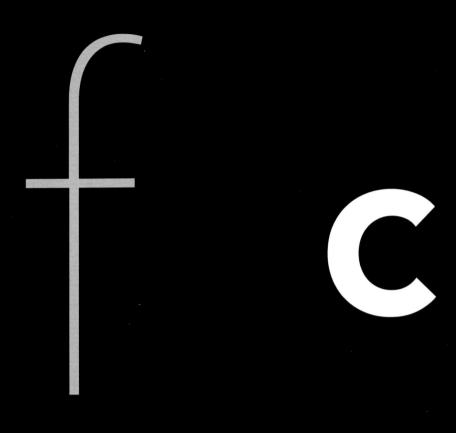

"Nothing you admire is perfect.
No electronic device, no hotel,
no steak has ever been perfect.
The work of the professional
is shipping. The professional
doesn't wait around for perfect."

Seth Godin, Entrepreneur,
Author, Squidoo.com Founder

Foundr tips

THE BEST WAY TO LEARN?

Dan Norris, WP Curve co-founder and author of *The 7 Day Startup*, lost count of the number of people who told him it was crazy to provide an unlimited service contract. But he had a theory on how he thought people would use the service, and instead of debating and theorizing, he put a few safeguards in place and launched. He discovered that he was right, which he learned by launching, not analyzing. Norris strongly believes that 99 percent of the problems he sees discussed in entrepreneur chat forums have already been solved by someone else. The other 1 percent is so easy to test that discussing the problem is useless compared to the effort required to get real data.

DAN NORRIS' QUICK, DIRTY, NO BS GUIDE TO A 7-DAY LAUNCH SCHEDULE

01 Throw out all of the validation attempts and theorizing and just launch something!

02 Focus all of your attention on what is working—do not waste time analyzing something that did not work or wondering if you should tweak something that is working.

03 The idea is either working or not working. If you have not tried hard enough, keep going. If it is anything other than that, stop.

USER FEEDBACK

Once your product or service is out there in the big, bad world—beyond a prototype, early adjustments, and full-on launch—the job of listening is still not done. The pros we spoke to emphasized just how important it is to keep the door open, and continue the conversation with the audience. Ongoing user feedback remains just as vital once things are in full swing as it was during the early days.

One of the things Jessica Livingston observed in her vast experience incubating new companies is that standout entrepreneurs create strong user feedback loops right from the outset, and are prepared to use that information to improve their products.

"You can't just lock yourself in a room, build some wonderful program, and then just expect it's going to work. You really have to be iterating on the product, showing it to users, asking them if they aren't using it then what would they change. Making sure every decision is what's best for the user experience is a really important quality."

Of course, there's another way to get instant feedback—become your own customer. Twitch founder Justin Kan recommended becoming an avid user of your own products, and taking your own feedback seriously. Recalling a time when several new ideas weren't gaining the traction he wanted to see, Kan said, in hindsight he wasn't talking to users, but he also wasn't using the products enough. To build something people really want, you need to do both.

"SHORTEN YOUR FEEDBACK CYCLE. BECOME YOUR OWN CUSTOMER. BUILD SOMETHING AND USE IT. IF IT SUCKS, CHANGE IT TO HOW YOU WANT. IF YOU DO THAT ENOUGH, YOU WILL ACTUALLY BUILD SOMETHING THAT PEOPLE WANT."

Justin Kan

WHEN TO GIVE UP

When it comes to knowing whether you're onto a winner or not, there's a fine line between determination and knowing when you're beating a dead horse, said YC's Jessica Livingston.

"One question we get a lot from founders who are struggling is when to ditch an idea. It's a very tough question. No one ever knows 100 percent what the answer is, but if you can't get anyone interested in using your product or you don't have something that's much better than what's out there already, it could be time to think of alternatives. But if you are using your product and it's really solving a need for you, or if you have a small group of people using it, it might not be time yet. It's a delicate balance."

JESSICA LIVINGSTON

When AOL co-founder Steve Case was among the many finding their way in the early days of web, you can only imagine the difficulty of knowing whether you were on the brink of a smash hit, or about to meet the fate of Pets.com. After all, as AOL blazed the trail for social media with its instant messaging and chat rooms, there wasn't much evidence of what would or wouldn't stick. For Case, it ultimately came down to his conviction in the idea itself.

"Sometimes, ideas turn out to not be so interesting, or there just isn't a market acceptance of them. In that case, it really is better to call it a day and figure out something else to do. But if you still believe in the idea, and you still believe there is a strategy to help take that idea and give it life, to give it scale, and you have an understanding of the competitor dynamics and you think it is possible to break through, then I think that argues for perseverance.

"Keep your focus on your team, your priorities, the broader competitive landscape and what partnerships might accelerate your growth—I think that's where it makes sense to stay the course. But keep tweaking what you're doing to reflect what the market is telling you."

Sometimes though, as Case suggests, the market just isn't there. For *Shark Tank* investor Robert Herjavec, it's a matter of looking at your numbers—growth potential, or lack thereof—as the most decisive factor when considering whether to cut and run or stay the course.

"You either grow or you die—we don't have a choice. If we don't grow, we're moving backwards and we're going out of business. There's a great saying by Andy Grove, 'Only the paranoid survive.' I'm not sure that applies just to technology; it applies to everything. We're very paranoid. But sometimes, if your market is dying and people are giving away your market share, and you don't want to do it anymore, there's nothing wrong with giving up and starting again.

starting again.

robert herjavec

Robin Chase Keeps the Customer in the Driver's Seat

Featured
in Issue 46
- *Driving
The Shared
Economy with
Robin Chase*

Founder
Robin Chase

Job
Co-founder of Zipcar

Success Story
Zipcar created a revolutionary business model in the early days of the sharing economy and challenged the concept of car ownership, rising to become a world leader in transportation.

A classic early entrepreneur's mistake is to surround yourself with co-founders and friends, all convinced that you've created the perfect product, only to find out you have no idea what customers really want.

The truth is, the only person who can tell you for sure whether or not they'd be willing to put down money for what you're offering is your customer. The only way you're going to build a great product is by communicating directly with your user.

Anything else and you're just assuming, and you know what they say about assuming.

In the fall of 1999, Robin Chase had a lightbulb moment when her co-founder told her about an interesting story of some people sharing a car in Berlin. Taken with the idea, within six months they had launched Zipcar.

▼

Despite the fact that there was only one car in operation when they started, a green Volkswagen beetle named "Betsy," Zipcar had proven itself almost immediately. The website was easy to use and the process simple enough for anyone to understand.

The reason it went so smoothly is that Chase was already intimately familiar with what her customers wanted out of the experience—she was her own customer.

"This is what I personally want to have. That I had three children, and a husband, and one car and I lived in a city. And I wanted a car sometimes, but I definitely did not want to own another car."

Today, Zipcar is one of the largest car-sharing services in the world, found in almost every major city, with over a million users and 13,000 cars.

It's a huge success. But let's contrast this with Chase's first startup venture after Zipcar, a long-distance ride-sharing business that ran into problems as soon as it launched.

"At that time I thought, 'Oh I'm really clever, I know a lot about transportation, I know I'm going to make this fancy website.' I spent a lot of money building this website and it was way, way, way too clever, so by the time it hit consumers, I had overbuilt it. So we spent the first three months un-building it."

Unlike the immediate success she experienced with Zipcar, Chase instead found that she had overestimated her users' ability to navigate her new website. Instead of reaching out to her customers and asking for their feedback, she made the classic mistake of assuming that she knew what her customer wanted.

"I would have thought that, at a minimum, to share a ride you would have to put in the time of day you're leaving, the time of day you're going to get there, origin, and destination, and how many seats you wanted to rent, and the price. That was too much. People were not interested in putting all of those details in."

The process was too complex, not intuitive enough, and instead all it did was serve to frustrate her initial users.

The lesson here is that no matter how much you know, at the end of the day, you're not an expert when it comes to your product. Your customer is the expert.

Lisa Q. Fetterman

Got a Kickstart From Devoted Early Adopters

Featured in
Issue 29 -
*Ingredients of
Success: Lisa
Q. Fetterman's
Journey from
the Kitchen to
a Crowdfunded
Triumph*

Founder
Lisa Q. Fetterman

Job
Co-founder and CEO of Nomiku

Success Story
Nomiku crowdfunded its way to more than $1 million to provide home chefs everywhere with a highly sought after *sous vide* machine. Fetterman's creation was the first of its kind on the market.

When we talk about early adopters we're not talking about your first batch of customers. We're talking about the people who truly love your product, flaws and all.

These people are so important in any business, regardless of the niche, because early adopters are always going to be your most valuable customers. They are going to be the most vocal, the most supportive, and most importantly, your early adopters aren't going to be afraid to tell you what you can do better.

To understand how to harness the power of early adopters, all you need to do is take a look at the story of Lisa Q. Fetterman.

Fetterman is the co-founder of a marvelous device known as the Nomiku. It's a *sous vide* machine, a device beloved by professional chefs, but that few home chefs would have heard of back when the company got started.

Traditionally, these machines were known to be clunky and extremely expensive, really only used in restaurants. Fetterman wanted a cheaper option so, along with her co-founder and now-husband, she built one. The result was a Frankenstein-like contraption that was made out of duct tape, an aquarium bubbler, a chopstick, and a PID machine, and the prototype of the Nomiku was born.

▼

Realizing she was onto something, Fetterman immediately began looking for others who would be interested in having their own *sous vide.*

"How do we get this out to more people who are like-minded? We just went on Twitter, put it out there: 'Hey who wants a *sous vide* machine?' We'd go to random people's houses, like cheese makers, and make them a *sous vide* machine to help them make cheese," she says. "I went to food blogs and I wanted them to try it out; I called up chefs around San Francisco to try our prototype."

that any home chef could put to work.

But Fetterman wasn't done leveraging the power of her early adopters quite yet.

Taking to Kickstarter to crowdfund the production of the Nomiku, she reached out to all of her initial customers and asked them to pledge. The result was the highest funded Kickstarter campaign in the food category at the time, raising nearly $600,000 within 30 days.

Because of the enthusiasm of those early customers, Nomiku blew away its crowdfunding goals in two Kickstarter campaigns. Word-of-mouth spread and soon it seemed everyone was talking about getting their own *sous vide* machine.

Today, the Nomiku can be found in kitchens all around the world, from ordinary homes, to Michelin-starred restaurants and even the White House. So much of that success was thanks to the support of Nomiku's adoring early adopters.

By no means did she have a polished product, but by getting in touch with her target users, she slowly began to build a community around her homemade prototype. In the midst of the foodie revolution, Fetterman managed to strike a chord.

By building this group of early adopters, Fetterman started gathering invaluable feedback on the Nomiku's design and functionality. By taking on their criticism, and showing that she was taking them seriously, the Nomiku developed a band of incredibly loyal customers.

The result was a beautifully designed *sous vide* machine

chapter 03
PEOPLE

Culture is the engine room of your organization. It's the beating heart, that often intangible quality that unites people with purpose, inspires their loyalty, and galvanizes them to do whatever it takes to achieve success.

Research also suggests that the ROI of a strong culture and happy employees can be measured in dollars. A 2011 study at the London School of Economics found that culture-building activities that promoted wellbeing represented a substantial annual ROI of more than 9 to 1, with increased productivity and reduced absenteeism.

Mindvalley CEO Vishen Lakhiani is the man standing at the intersection of mindfulness and business, and he knows workplace culture. With Mindvalley HQ voted by readers of *Inc. Magazine* as one of the World's Coolest Offices in 2012, he has it down to a fine art. The company not only boasts several hundred geographically dispersed employees, but has also attracted more than a million subscribers and 300,000 paying customers.

Building a winning culture, Lakhiani said, is about so much more than just stocking a staff fridge with food and drinks.

CULTURE

03 PEOPLE

"That's not culture; those are perks. Culture is an underlying set of beliefs and habits that your people possess. These beliefs and habits define who you are. Culture hacking is important because people take on the beliefs and habits of the people they are close to. The more people with healthy beliefs and habits, the greater your culture."

Lakhiani encourages founders to get their teams together on a semi-regular basis to discuss a code of values. This will not only help you shape the habits and beliefs you want your company to have, but will help to inform your broader business strategy. "The code becomes a decision-making mechanism, helping you make decisions faster, while protecting your values."

In this sense, culture is also about more than just keeping your team happy. It's about establishing the very foundation on which success or failure is built. As a testament to its importance, legendary advertising executive Alex Bogusky puts it even before branding, his very bread-and-butter.

"Everyone wants me to work on branding. But branding doesn't work until you've got everything else working. You can't just put **lipstick** on a pig. A lot of my work involved juicing a company from within, or helping them understand how to see themselves and to create a **culture of success.**"

ALEX BOGUSKY

That doesn't mean, however, that the people-pleasing side of culture isn't important. Canva CEO Melanie Perkins believes that making people feel included, valued, and cared for is central to business performance, including encouraging people to spend quality time together. At Canva offices, group lunches provide the perfect opportunity to foster a meaningful connection with colleagues, with the team sharing meals prepared by one of three chefs employed by the company.

Foundr has a ton of admiration for the late **Dave Goldberg, former SurveyMonkey CEO,** who tragically passed away in 2015. One of his many areas of expertise was company culture, and Goldberg once told Foundr that part of the practice is simply being nice.

"When I first moved to L.A. to work in the music business, one of my friends said to me, 'You know, you're a nice guy. Just remember that. This is a town filled with people that aren't that nice.' He's like, 'Be nice to everybody.'"

DAVE Goldberg

Building a kickass team is one of the most repeated pieces of wisdom told to Foundr by leading entrepreneurs. It comes up again and again. And it's a theory backed up by some weighty research—according to Deloitte's Human Capital Trends 2016 Report, building a high-performing "network of teams" is one of the best ways to boost performance.

As Justin's Peanut Butter founder Justin Gold discovered on his journey to operating a multimillion-dollar business, the most effective way to build a team was to hire people smarter than himself, and give them the opportunity to lead.

03 PEOPLE

BUILDING A TEAM

"My approach was to hire people with great experience, who knew the industry and knew how to grow my company in ways that I never could. I brought on people smarter than I was, and I let them lead. I gave them guardrails, because I had a vision and knew where I wanted to go, but I let them lead."

● ● ●

This is a common refrain among successful business founders, who all seem to have learned very early on that hiring a bunch of yes men, or people who won't challenge or even outperform you is a fast route to mediocrity. For Rod Drury of Xero, that also means recruiting for a variety of skills, work styles, and personalities.

"It's not about hiring people just like yourself. It's about trying to build diversity. High-performing teams need a whole range of skills, so build that unique collection of people who together can be awesome."

● ● ●

We're often sold a story about great startups being the product of one visionary leader. But in reality, it's a strong vision, along with a chorus of other perspectives. AOL Co-founder Steve Case noted the importance of balancing the different voices, while keeping a firm eye on the future.

"Recognize that entrepreneurship is a team sport. It's not just about the founder or founders, it's about a broader mix of people. You have to strike the right balance between having a team of people who work well together and having distinct and diverse perspectives. If you just focus on people you like to work with, chances are, it's not going to give you the different perspectives you need."

"At the same time, if you just focus on having different skill sets, and don't think about how to mold them together as a team, that's not going to work either. So it's a tricky balance, in terms of getting in front of the curve, putting the teams in place to manage where you're going, not where you are, and certainly not where you've been."

Even if you're fully on board with the importance of weaving together a diverse set of people into your team, that doesn't mean it's always easy to tell from a resume or an interview if they're the right fit. Robin Chase learned this lesson this while growing Zipcar into the world's largest car sharing service, and emphasized the importance of testing out new hires first.

"The people you hire in the early days have to be problem solvers, people who will scramble together and figure out how to do something themselves—because you don't have any money. It's a really good idea to hire people hourly before you hire them full time. They are so critically important, you don't have time to make a mistake. This way you will know: Can they do these things? Do we have good chemistry? Are they a can-do person? Before you make that commitment."

ROBIN CHASE

One way to test out that chemistry, suggested Buffer CEO Joel Gascoigne, is to consider a starter trial period to allow your business and each new employee to size up cultural and job fit. At Buffer, the hiring process includes a 45-day trial or "bootcamp," which is a two-way street to ensure both parties are happy. "About 70 percent of the time, it's a good fit," Gascoigne said.

JOEL GASCOIGNE

Steve Mehr's Top 3 Tips for Building a Team

Steve Mehr is the founder and CEO of consulting and advertising agency Webshark 360. Mehr is a branding pro, but he also offered Foundr some keen insights into the hiring process.

1

Put aside your ego:
Know where your skill set ends. Mehr is a builder, but a horrible manager. Find someone better than you.

2

Hire hungry people:
A lot of entrepreneurs are afraid to hire ambitious people, for fear that they'll try to take over. Put that fear aside. "I want someone working for me that wants my job. Because if he or she's willing to do what I do, then they can have my job."

3

Don't give too much control to unproven leaders:
It's your ship, so make sure the wrong person isn't at the helm.

trust

"You don't lead by hitting people over the head—that's assault, not leadership."

DWIGHT **D. EISENHOWER**

It's funny because it's true, Ike. But it's not always a laughing matter. Being a micromanager, or someone who doesn't give people the freedom to execute their roles, is a great way to get people bolting out the back door. But it is such an easy trap to fall into, especially when, as founder, you're used to being involved in every decision. There's also a good chance you have a lot more on the line than the people working for you.

This is a pitfall that dozens of elite entrepreneurs warned us about. Remember that having room to stretch their legs creatively is what gets people out of bed in the morning. And if you heeded that great advice from Justin Gold and Rod Drury, you've hired some really smart folks!

Allowing people creative freedom has always been at the heart of Richard Branson's management style, with the Virgin boss explaining that your ability to trust people is directly tied to your effectiveness as a leader. "I believe a good leader brings out the best in people by listening to them, trusting them, believing in them, respecting them, and letting them have a go."

There's also the fact that, in the startup environment, the people who will be drawn to your business, and those who will thrive within it, often don't do so hot within a rigid structure. Otherwise, they'd be working 9-to-5 at the local fill-in-the-blank. As founder of The Grid Dan Tocchini told Foundr, that means considering what he would want in a work setting.

dan tocchini

"We give people control over their domain and a lot of freedom, which is really important. I know for myself, if I had a really structured environment, I wouldn't thrive. I would break the rules. So we look for those kind of people. We also give them really difficult problems and tell them to just go and figure it out. They can employ whatever they want to, as long as they figure it out. You need to let people just run with it."

An important part of being a trusting leader is embracing delegation, assigning work to others with the faith that they'll competently handle things without your meddling. That can mean simply moving tasks and duties from off your plate over to someone else's, but for Collis Ta'eed, the founder of online marketplace giant Envato, it has to go much further than that if you want to take things to the next level.

"In the early days, delegating for me was much more about giving directions. Now, as Envato has gotten bigger and the team more senior, I delegate better. I say: Here's the context, now how do we get there? It's also about flexibility. I used to believe the hours a person worked was really important, which is a bit of a trap. Results and outcomes are actually more significant, not just how busy someone looks."

"Always treat your team like human beings and encourage employees to do other stuff outside of what they are doing in work. I also encourage my staff to talk back to me to tell me when they think I'm wrong. You don't want to surround yourself with sycophants. Your team is there to challenge and inspire."

DAVID BRIM
CO-FOUNDER & CEO OF
TOMCAR AUSTRALIA

Vishen Lakhiani on How to Create an Exceptional Company Culture

"Culture hacking is important because people take on the beliefs and habits of the people they are close to. You have to define your beliefs." Mindvalley's Vishen Lakhiani shares his top advice for getting culture right.

1

Establish a company code of beliefs:
On a semi-regular basis, get your team together and figure out your code of values. This will help you not only shape the right habits and beliefs you want your company to have, but it will help govern business strategy.

2

When hiring, hire for beliefs:
If you're a small startup, or a solopreneur looking to take someone on, this is the most vital consideration. Each new employee comes with their own set of beliefs. Do they share your beliefs about what a company is and what a company should be? Mindvalley leaves nothing to chance, by presenting a quiz to new employees to analyze such beliefs before any new hires meet with HR.

3

Create a culture that helps evolve healthy beliefs and habits:
Make your values clear to each employee, especially new hires. Your beliefs make up your reality. But remember, beliefs are moldable. If an employee believes something unhealthy like the need to work a 70-hour week, you can change this with a little perseverance.

Polina Raygorodskaya
Invited Experts On Board

Featured in
Issue 45 -
Just the Ticket

Founder
Polina Raygorodskaya

Job
Co-founder and CEO of Wanderu

Success Story
Since launching in 2013, Raygorodskaya's travel booking company Wanderu has shaken up ground transportation, gracing many "best of" lists, and topping 2 million monthly users.

A key part of being an entrepreneur is knowing both your strengths and areas where you need to improve. In an ideal world, you would have plenty of time to sharpen the dull spots, but an ideal world it is not.

So what do you do when you need to move fast, but you're missing important skills or knowledge related to your industry? The solution is to build a great team of people around you, whether they're advisers, co-founders, or employees.

When Polina Raygorodskaya first came up with the idea for Wanderu, she sought to create an online database that allowed travelers to easily find and book bus and train tickets. At the time, there wasn't anything like it, and consumers were forced to visit every company's individual website and manually compare their options.

While she had the marketing and PR chops down, Raygorodskaya knew right away that in order to turn her idea into a reality, she needed someone with the technical expertise to round out her team. She chose longtime friend Igor Bratnikov to be her technical co-founder and help her build the Wanderu platform.

▼

However, they soon encountered another problem: a lack of expertise when it came to the transportation industry.

"We learned quickly that in order for us to succeed in this industry, we should bring on advisers that know this industry very well, that can help get us up to speed and be there for us when we have questions, or if we need guidance."

By getting in contact with industry leader Craig Lentzsch, Raygorodskaya was able to bring someone on board with more than 20 years of knowledge, experience, and contacts within the transportation sector. He was exactly the kind of person Wanderu needed if it was going to revolutionize such a complex industry.

From there, it was a matter of reaching out to other experts and asking them to join on as advisers.

"I do highly recommend startups to have advisers. Usually, the way it works is, you give them a little bit of equity in exchange for specific things you want that adviser to do, whether that's coaching you, making introductions, or just talking to you several times a month. You don't want to have too many, but a handful is always helpful."

Raygorodskaya already knew her target market extremely well. After all, she was a seasoned traveler herself, having crossed the country many times and held dozens of conversations with fellow passengers about their many woes. But she didn't know much about the workings of the ground transportation industry—a tangle of large, established companies.

While this lack of industry knowledge might scare away some entrepreneurs, Raygorodskaya set out to find someone with the expertise she was looking for.

"One of the first things we did when we started Wanderu was that we brought on the former CEO of Greyhound, which is the largest bus company within the United States. We brought him on as an adviser."

By building such a strong team of people around her, Raygorodskaya was able to focus on building Wanderu by using her own strengths, knowing that she could comfortably rely upon the knowledge and skills of others where she was less experienced.

It's led to tremendous success. Growing roughly 400 percent quarter-over-quarter after its launch, and building a network of partners that spans across the United States, Canada, and Mexico, Wanderu is now the largest company of its kind in North America.

chapter 04

MARKETING

Love Thy Customer

In today's social and digital media-fueled marketing battleground, customers are holding the wheel to a degree few experts really saw coming. Over the past few years, marketers have simply been focused on getting big, shiny digital campaigns out there, to be seen and engaged with.

Engagement alone no longer cuts it, nor is it a good enough measure on its own of your marketing impact. Making your customers happy at every turn is paramount, which is why expressions like "customer obsessed" are popping up in brand books everywhere.

Tony Robbins became a household name as the man who popularized life coaching. With a client list that features Oprah Winfrey and Bill Clinton, Robbins is a powerful global brand, a man who has offered wisdom to more than 50 million people in 100 countries. When it comes to marketing success, Robbins said falling in love with your clients is the single most important thing you can do.

"Don't fall in love with your product or your service, because will become outdated. You can make money screwing somebody but you can't be weal and stay wealthy unl you continue to find to add more value th anybody else does, a that means it never s To do that, you need love your clients."

TONYROBBINS

juliahartz

Offering top notch service, while cultivating real relationships, is more important than ever. That's why Eventbrite's **Julia Hartz** said she learned some of her most valuable lessons in her early role as the company's customer service contact.

● ● ●

"Really understanding your customers comes from building relationships with them. It's important to be their best friend, therapist, family member. I would spend countless hours on email and on the phone. We still get calls from early customers who have our cell phone numbers, and who I would consider family members at this point. It worked because we honored what they were asking for. We unpacked their feedback, we listened, we took it all in."

But it's not just about customer loyalty. **Tom Bilyeu** told Foundr how a "customer first" approach gave Quest Nutrition negotiating firepower with large-scale retailers. In Bilyeu's experience, holding off on negotiating major distribution contracts until they had built a powerful customer demand was a tactical masterstroke.

"You want to establish a relationship with your customer directly. Don't go to stores first—that was a big decision for us. By going direct to the consumer, building a community online, socially, making sure your product is really resonating with people, you create something called pull-through demand. So we had stores and distributors coming to us, rather than the other way around, and that put us in a position where we could really get more favorable, balanced contracts. This has been incredibly important to the success of our brand."

TOM BILYEU

04 MARKETING

CONTENT MARKETING

Now that you're thinking warm and fuzzy thoughts about your customers, the next step is to consider the content you serve up to keep them curious and engaged. From blog posts and podcasts to videos, case studies, top-10 lists and infographics, there's a stack of content marketing options to sink your teeth into, as well as plenty of modern apps and tools to help you create them.

When it comes to content marketing cut through, the world's top entrepreneurs have told us repeatedly that if you want to make an impact, give readers—and search engines—what they want: original, high-quality content, focused on topics that are relevant to your business. Do this right, and your desired audience will beat a path to your door.

Chris Brogan's business design company, Human Business Works, publishes *Owner* magazine, while Brogan himself has worked with iconic brands like Disney, Motorola, Coke, PepsiCo, Microsoft, and Google. When it comes to content marketing, he still believes the humble blog is the most effective way for people to get to know your business.

"There's really almost no company that shouldn't have some kind of a blog. It's free mind-reading, meaning your potential prospects can read how you think about ideas and projects. They'll get a better sense of what you're going to do."

Brogan went on to call blogging a form of "weaponized storytelling" that helps businesses earn their stripes by solving problems for potential customers:

"You fill the blanks in with content marketing. Content marketing is a technique of creating and distributing valuable, relevant, and consistent content to attract and acquire a clearly defined audience, with the objective of driving profitable customer action. Publishing content to the web can bring in customers who you would never otherwise have met. I call it weaponized storytelling. Think 'How can I come alongside somebody who might have the use of this product or service, and tell the story such that they see themselves in it?'"

Another running theme in successful content marketing (and one that we here at Foundr are especially devoted to) is the idea of providing value every time, in a variety of ways. Content needs to serve a purpose of its own, and not just land a sale, said Tom Bilyeu, protein bar empire co-founder.

"We put a ton of energy and resources behind not just creating good content, but creating a wide variety of content we think will be super supportive to all the people in the Quest community. That's everything from Facebook live, to live cooking shows, to Inside Quest podcast, which is bringing on incredible thought leaders, and getting them to come on and tell their story. It just makes a lot of sense to us. Inside Quest also doesn't generate any revenue. We don't try to sell anything, there's no advertising. It's literally just a give back to our community of fans who've been so supportive of the brand."

However, as Buffer Co-founder and CEO Joel Gascoigne reminded us, not everyone will sign up the first time they hear about your product or service. Your content marketing aim should therefore be to generate buzz as often and as early as you can, in order to nudge potential customers in the right direction. "I now believe that when building a startup, as much early focus should be put on marketing and customer development as on product development."

"Give people value. Make them laugh. You don't need a business objective for every piece of creative."

Gary Vaynerchuk
Entrepreneur, Author, Investor, Speaker

Darren Rowse's Top Five Content Tips

ProBlogger founder and content extraordinaire Darren Rowse shared with Foundr his best advice for creating incredible content:

1. KNOW YOUR READER

The first step is to think about who your reader is, and then think about how you want to change your reader with your content. Consider what is interesting to them.

2. CREATE CONTENT TO SOLVE PROBLEMS

What are their pain points? Create content that's going to eliminate pain in the lives of those you want to read your content.

3. PUSH IT ACTIVELY

If you're just starting out, it's really important not to have a "build it and they will come" mentality, because readers won't come no matter how good it is. You need to be pushing it out there.

4. NETWORK DELIBERATELY

Identify the top three content creators in your niche. Then ask yourself, "How can I build a useful presence on those blogs, on those Facebook pages, in those podcasts?"

5. USE SEO BEST PRACTICES, BUT DON'T OVERDO IT

Understand the basics of SEO, but don't let that determine what you write. I don't do anything to manipulate search results. I'm just trying to be a good citizen of the web and produce the best content that I can.

● ● ●

Eugene Woo's Content Marketing Growth Hacks

Infographic service Venngage exploded in popularity in a short amount of time, with traffic growing by five times in a few years. Co-founder Eugene Woo explained their outreach-focused approach to content marketing.

1. YOU CAN'T JUST BLOG:

"When you write and you're not a brand name and no one cares about you, you don't have a following, nothing happens. No one's coming, no one's sharing." It's all about outreach to get the word out.

2. QUALITY, NOT QUANTITY:

Woo's team does serious networking to get other sites to mention and link back to Venngage and the content it produces. They'll work harder to get high-quality, relevant mentions and put the time into making unique and valuable content.

3. OFFER SOMETHING:

When trying to get the word out, offer something in exchange for a mention. In their case, it was a free infographic. "Especially if you're really small—you're not a brand name, you're not famous, why would someone want to mention you, unless it's a win-win?"

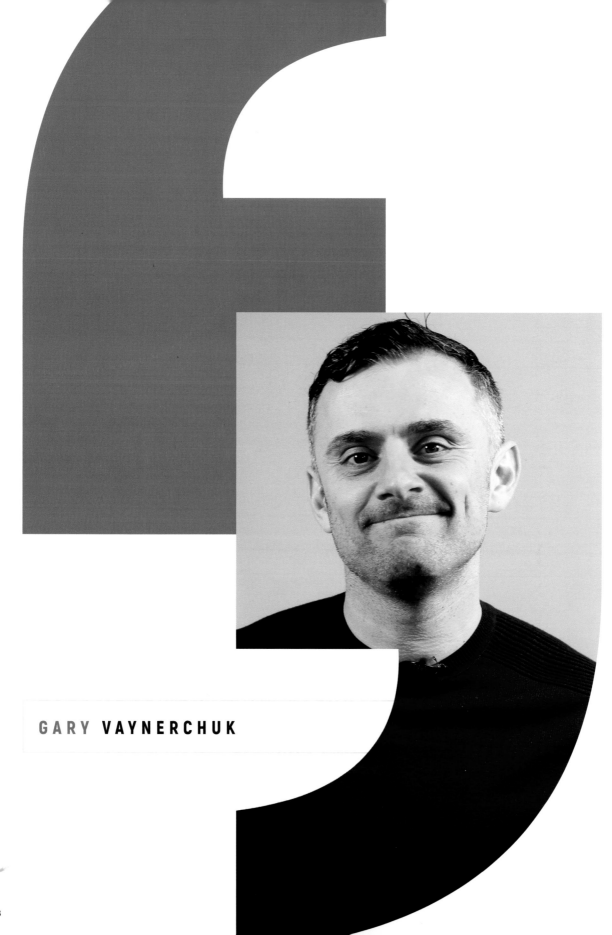

GARY **VAYNERCHUK**

04 MARKETING
STORYTELLING

To be an effective marketer in today's economy, you need finely honed storytelling chops. Not tall tales or fantastic fables, but the honest, authentic stories customers are looking for as a reason to connect with you.

Industry celebrity, *New York Times*-bestselling author, and purveyor of the hustle, Gary Vaynerchuk, knows a thing or two about spinning a good yarn. Having built a 1.3 million-strong Twitter following by using his storytelling abilities to connect with people, Vaynerchuk told Foundr:

"The marketing industry often operates five years in the past, with methods that don't work anymore. Just give people value. Quality storytelling always wins. It's not about pushing advertising. It's about bringing value."

michelle

From a practical standpoint, YouTube trailblazer and beauty product icon Michelle Phan encouraged founders to apply the same storytelling principles that are commonly used in literature, creating a narrative arc your readers can easily follow. Phan also offered a neat trick for sharpening your storytelling abilities:

— ● ● ● —

"You need to tell a story. Know your underlying theme and vision, and have a strong structure to execute your story—a beginning, middle, and an end. A natural storyteller just knows how to tell a story, but if you want to learn, my biggest recommendation would be to watch movie trailers. Movie trailers are a great way to learn. They tell an entire story in two minutes!"

Marie Forleo agreed, with the entrepreneur, philanthropist and TV host telling Foundr that a carefully constructed headline can be the difference between piquing someone's interest, or losing them within the first few seconds. Forleo too offered a creative tip for developing your storytelling prowess:

"Look at the magazine stand next time you are leaving the grocery store, and pay attention to how editors use headlines to get you to pick up their magazines. Listen to the news on the television or radio and pay attention to how they hook you to listen to the next segment.

When you're first starting out, you have to really pay attention to those headlines and subheadlines. Because let's face it, you can create the most amazing piece of content but if your headlines sucks, your email subject line sucks, or you don't know how to write a good social media update, you've lost."

MARIE FORLEO

04 MARKETING

Influencer Marketing

Using brand ambassadors has been a reliable marketing tactic since cigarette companies began using shiny-haired movie stars to sell cigarettes back in the 1940s. While formal ambassadors are still a marketing mainstay (nobody sells Nespresso like Clooney), the social-hybrid brand influencer model has become an increasingly powerful way to explode a fledgling brand.

It's word-of-mouth at its most potent. With a new breed of "social celebrity" amassing huge followings on sites like Instagram, customers are turning more and more to these very effective self-promoters to inform their own product choices. Influencer marketing, therefore, presents the ideal opportunity for brands to leverage these relationships and entice new followers.

Marketing superstar Gretta Rose van Riel was so certain that connecting to brand influencers was the way forward, she created an entire new product to support it. Nichify is a social network that links brands up with social influencers.

"With my product companies, I learned it takes a lot of time and energy to do influencer marketing. So Nichify was an organic progression around the want to systemize our own marketing. We launched six months ago and have grown really quickly, with almost a billion in social reach. It's a really great communications tool for brands to use to collaborate with social media influencers and talk to them in one place."

● ● ●

Shaun Neff follows the more traditional brand ambassador model, in which forging close links with key personalities in each of his retail markets has been an important strategy in an unforgiving industry. Collaborations with everyone from Snoop Dogg and Wiz Khalifa, to Disney and dozens of leading sporting personalities have kept Neff relevant to multiple audiences at once.

But the same principle holds true of aligning yourself with trusted personalities, and in Neff's mind, the people you associate your brand with is one of marketing's most critical success factors. "Nail these three important attributes on every campaign—a great product, a great marketing story, and a great ambassador."

Of course, there is a corner you can cut in influencer marketing—become an influencer. Internet celebrity Michelle Phan reminded founders to leverage their own personal brands and become key people of influence. You never know where it might lead.

"I knew that creating my YouTube channel would be valuable, because when you're an influencer and have people following you, it's always going to be valuable. I was studying at the time and I knew that if I had a good following and could show that, then someone might hire me over someone else with the same talent. I knew it could give me an edge, but I never thought in a million years that could become a multimillion-dollar business."

MICHELLE PHAN

04 MARKETING

SOCIAL MEDIA

Social media has truly changed the way we share and find information, news, products, business opportunities, you name it. In fact, social media has played a huge part in the growth of Foundr Magazine, and our ever-expanding media company. It has also had a profound impact on many of the entrepreneurs we've interviewed over the years, and we've included a couple of the savviest approaches to the subject here.

Hustle king Gary Vaynerchuk is one man who has proven the value of using social media as the building blocks of business, with his legions of loyal fans elevating Vaynerchuk's personal brand to cult figure status. When it comes to making a splash on social, he encourages founders to cast a wide net across multiple channels. "It's not enough to be master of one. In the social media space, better to be a jack of all trades and maximize exposure across all platforms to reach the largest possible audience."

However, while having a strong personal brand can be an effective strategy, marketing guru Guy Kawasaki believes the majority of your social heavy lifting should be done in aid of your company brand:

"If you're working for a startup, you should be building the brand's social media platform as opposed to the CEO's. Very few CEOs know how to use social media well. Maybe the only exception is Richard Branson. But CEOs come and go, believe it or not. The brand has to stay."

Kawasaki also offered some practical advice for founders who struggle with what to post on social media, which involves running content ideas through two simple tests before sharing them. The first, simply referred to as the "Re-Share Test" involves weighing up content in terms of its shareability. If you feel confident a piece of content is so useful, informative or entertaining that your followers will happily re-share it, it's a safe bet.

The second measure, Kawasaki's "NPR Test," uses the example of public radio stations, who, after providing valuable free content year round, often ask listeners to show their appreciation during an annual pledge drive. Such a strategy works, more often than not, because people feel obligated to reward the station for their great content. The value you build into your social channels can have a similar effect when it comes to promotions and product launches, Kawasaki said.

"As a business on social media, you need to provide great value, information, assistance, analysis and entertainment, so when you run promotions, people feel the need to reciprocate, or at least tolerate, what you're doing. The only reason you can get away with this is because every other day you're providing great content."

GUY KAWASAKI

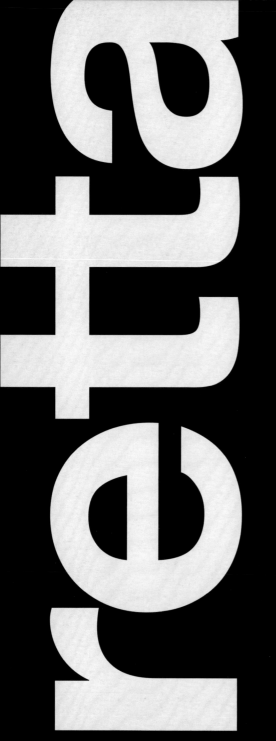

For Gretta Rose van Riel, who has a combined Instagram reach in excess of 15 million, building a social presence for multiple products at once meant stamping her authority across a number of popular topics within one platform. She essentially let her powerful social media presence, and the interests of the followers she's amassed, shape the direction of her products and marketing, as opposed to the other way around.

After identifying popular topics, van Riel set up Instagram pages targeted at the relevant audience demographics, and seeded them with regular, high-quality visual content. Once a vertical had attracted a significant follower base, van Riel launched a product catering to them—like DROP Bottle, a sleek range of designer water bottles created for van Riel's legions of "health" and "detox" followers.

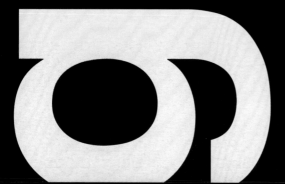

"Building up Instagram pages across verticals has been really, really helpful for us. Success definitely has a lot to do with your content strategy—not just identifying a product that's trending, but content that's trending in verticals around your product. Your focus should be content, engagement, growth, and then conversion. Start with content: look at what's popular in your industry or vertical, visit like-minded pages, see what's working and use it as a guide. Then move on to people engaging with that content, which might be starting off with some hashtags. Consistency and momentum are two of the biggest factors around recurring growth."

Gretta Rose van Riel

Tom Bilyeu

Profited by Giving Stuff Away

Featured in
Issue 44 -
*Building a
Unicorn*

● ● ●

Job
Co-founder and President of Quest Nutrition

Success Story
Quest went from a side project to a global health and wellness unicorn company, with 57,000 percent growth in its first three years, leading to a $1 billion valuation.

Tom Bilyeu had a crazy idea, a few of them actually.

He was a marketer, but had an obsession with fitness and health and decided to follow his passion. Crazy idea number one.

He then decided that he wanted to zone in on the uber-competitive and crowded market of fitness nutrition. Crazy idea number two.

Crazy idea number three? He wanted to make a protein bar, and compete against the dozens of other protein bar brands jostling furiously for a spot in the market.

Quite a proposition.

But if you are as talented as your ideas are crazy, sometimes they pay off. That's what happened with the resulting company, Quest Nutrition, founded by Bilyeu, Ron Penna, and Mike Osborn.

▼

A big part of Bilyeu and his team's success had to do with the fact they were addressing a real issue in fitness marketing. The most popular approach marketed in the fitness field is that of "eat less, train more," which only works for a narrow percentage of the population, and is also not a very appealing lifestyle choice.

Quest's founders reasoned that by taking the types of food people wanted to eat, and making them healthy and really good, they could bridge the gap between what the industry was dictating and what the average person was prepared to do to lead a healthier life.

After a lot of experimenting, the team came up with a delicious, low-sugar protein bar. Armed with a winning product, Bilyeu was ready to use his marketing skills to get the protein bar to the people.

One of Quest's initial strategies— to build direct relationships with customers—became a powerful proof point for their product, and one of the early calling cards of the brand. As a group of seasoned marketers compelled by a belief in the power of community, they built a groundswell of early momentum by applying a mixture of modern and traditional marketing tactics.

For one, part of his company's marketing strategy was to give away a ton of stuff—from diet plans, to exercise regimens and, of course, loads of free protein bars.

Because the product was good, and the founders had a sincere and open approach, giving stuff away drew useful customer feedback and invaluable word-of-mouth marketing.

"We were literally giving away the product saying, 'Tell us if you like it and tell us if you hate it. We want to know.'" Bilyeu says. "We had a very different approach that got a lot of people excited. Not just about the product, but they felt good about the way we treated them."

What this ultimately did was create an online community of people raving about Quest bars and the Quest brand. This generated huge consumer-side demand, which put Bilyeu in a strong position when it came to negotiating with retailers. Sure shelves were already crowded with protein bars, but retailers had customers banging on their doors demanding they stock up on Quest.

For Bilyeu, giving away free product was central to his marketing strategy and the company's long-term success. He didn't view it as a drain on funds— he saw it as an investment.

"It was sacrificing profit if you think about the amount of money you make on each dollar. But think about the amount of money you're putting in your bank account. I'd rather make 10 percent profit and put a billion dollars in my bank account, than make 90 percent profit and put a hundred dollars in my bank account."

Gary Vaynerchuk Knows How to Get Your Attention

Featured in
Issue 36 -
*Your Attention,
Please*

Founder
Gary Vaynerchuk

● ● ●

Job
Co-founder of VaynerMedia, investor, speaker, and bestselling author

Success Story
Gary V built his family's wine business into a $60 million company right out of college, then went on to become a successful investor and marketing guru. One of his bestselling books is marketing staple *Jab, Jab, Jab, Right Hook*.

If you had to choose one word to characterize the internet, what would it be?

Communication? Innovation? Cats?

Try volume.

The amount of information, notifications, videos, flashes, and twinkles going on in the world of the web can overwhelm the most meditative monk.

For an entrepreneur, this can actually be bad news. Your success is dependent on getting people to pay attention, then converting that attention into a purchase.

Sure you have access to far more people thanks to the internet, but how do you break through all of the noise and get your budding business noticed? Gary Vaynerchuk was one of the first marketers to carefully articulate this problem, and offer some effective solutions.

His secret? Well, for one, he can really hustle. Vaynerchuk doesn't consider himself especially talented, but he really moves, working between 15 to 16 hours a day. It allows him to cover a lot of bases and have a presence across a lot of channels. He's a believer in maximizing exposure across all platforms to reach the largest audience possible.

But Gary V is probably most famous for his Jab, Jab, Jab, Right Hook approach to online marketing. People get hung up on the ratio of jabs to hooks, but the essence of this strategy is, to gain a following online, you have to give much more value than what you ask of people. If you aren't providing something that people value or enjoy, they'll tune you out.

▼

You can see this in action with Vaynerchuk's Wine Library TV, where his online success all began. It was a video blog he started when YouTube was still a 1-year-old internet debutante. He was just a guy working at a wine shop in New Jersey, but started posting videos that were, more than anything, entertaining. They were unusual and fun, with his frenzied enthusiasm and mad energy undercutting the stuffy world of wine connoisseurs. The videos drew enough attention that he ended up on network shows like *Late Night with Conan O'Brien* and *The Ellen DeGeneres Show.*

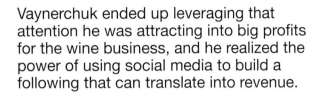

Vaynerchuk ended up leveraging that attention he was attracting into big profits for the wine business, and he realized the power of using social media to build a following that can translate into revenue.

"Give people value. Make them laugh. You don't need a business objective for every piece of creative."

These days he has millions following him on nearly every major social network. Vaynerchuk operates the agency VaynerMedia and helps clients reach more people and new heights in sales. He still stresses the importance of storytelling over pushing advertising. Promotion should be delivered sparingly. Give away your best stuff away for free, and then sprinkle in some ads tastefully.

If there's one more lesson from Vaynerchuk's rise, it's to love what you do. That's the underlying secret behind that mad enthusiasm people saw in Wine Library TV, and for that endless hustle that allows him to get his name out there.

He loves the game of business. He's addicted to it. Is it even hustle if you love it?

For entrepreneurs making their first forays into social media, take a moment and consider how much you love what you are promoting. Because you're going to have to love it a lot to hustle enough to make it.

chapter 05
BRAND

BUILDING A BRAND

This leads us to the living and breathing element that is your brand. It's fair to say that the digital revolution has flipped the branding game on its head, with today's playbook reading very differently than that of just five years ago.

Brands that are still clutching onto their traditional media plans and maintaining the impenetrable wall between themselves and their customers are losing ground, fast. Meanwhile, younger digital native brands are growing legions of loyal fans by adopting a more accessible, human approach.

The reality is, in this customer-led economy, most of us have come to expect seamless, meaningful experiences from our chosen brands. While it's not a total "baby out with the bathwater" scenario—enduring principles of branding like finding your audience and nailing a consistent tone of voice still apply—the startups rocketing ahead are the ones that can successfully turn this people-powered momentum into sales fuel.

As a founder, perhaps one with limited exposure to marketing, it can all seem like one big riddle. But here's a good place to start: *Branding is a lot more than just a few snappy visuals and a tag line.* It encapsulates every imprint of your product or service, and every interaction a potential customer has with you. For Richard Branson, branding is the X-factor that gives your business a leg up.

"I believe that a great company, whether improving a sector or creating a new one, needs to have an excellent product or service at its core, needs strong management to execute the plan, and a good brand to give it the edge over its competitors."

Part of the reason developing a good brand is so tricky is the fact that it's not a one-time job, but more of a constellation of decisions that form a larger shape over a long time. The North Face is a classic example of how this can unfold—the company steadily laid a foundation made of little bits of almost folk legend, which established a reputation of superb quality and reliability, former CEO Hap Klopp said.

"Brands are like coral; they build on a whole bunch of different points and come together in an elegant way down the road. But while you are building them, it's hard to see, and their impact doesn't really come together instantly but over time. Brands come from consistency and patience and from using novel and innovative ways to shout your message out to the marketplace."

It's also a process that never ends, as a good brand must always be evolving to stay relevant. That doesn't mean constantly overhauling all of your materials, but it does mean keeping an eye down the road. This is especially true in the fashion business, as Shaun Neff can attest.

"The hardest part of growing a brand is putting out something that's different to what already exists. Our brand has been out there for over 10 years now and kids know it. So now the challenges come in Neff continuing to be a leader. But I think we've done a phenomenal job of staying relevant and ahead of the curve. Part of what we do is go out there with things we believe in or think are rad, and try to start these trends. We're trying to be a thumbprint of youth culture, which allows us to test a lot of different artists, genres, and collaborations. If you can make the majority of them sticky, you're good."

05 BRAND

FINDING YOUR NICHE

If you're lucky, your product or service has a natural niche audience. Or you might have to dig a little deeper to find it. Either way, immersing yourself in one or even multiple subcultures is a powerful, proven brand-building activity.

The great news is that social media has now made subcultures more accessible to you than ever before, as demonstrated by Michelle Phan, who dove right into the world of makeup and beauty with nothing but an internet connection.

"There's going to be a niche market that's going to love and enjoy what you love. It might not be mainstream or mass market, but the internet has given people the capabilities to reach a niche market. And the word niche has evolved—it doesn't mean something small anymore. Niche can mean 10 million viewers; it can mean massive followings."

michelle phan

daymond

john

Once you have identified your niche, creating hype is one of the best ways to get your brand on everyone's lips, as branding expert and investor **Daymond John** discovered when he launched **FUBU**. The streetwear brand, which stands for For Us By Us, was first created as a label for lovers of hip-hop to wear proudly, at a time when major retailers like Timberland were trying to distance themselves from the scene.

"It was for kids who loved this new music called hip-hop, that came with a way to walk, talk, and dress—a lifestyle. We decided we would be proud of the people **who purchased our clothes.** Young people, people of color, hip-hop lovers—here was a brand they could identify with and make an emotional connection with."

DAYMOND **JOHN**

This concept has become even more powerful as the internet has made it easier to pull in significant numbers from a very specific target market, without having to become a pop culture sensation. Self-help guru **Tim Ferriss** has built his massive career on this principle, never worrying about achieving mainstream success, and instead carving out reliable chunks of the market and focusing his efforts.

"You do not need to appeal to the entire world. If you try to appeal to everyone, you'll get nowhere. It's too expensive and it doesn't work. Define specific target numbers. Mine were ten to twenty thousand books per week, and I knew I could achieve that if I targeted my demographic correctly. So I would ask myself, who are these people and where are they already going?"

TIM FERRISS

05 BRAND

CREATING A CONNECTION

Building a brand today also requires a human touch and good dose of authenticity. This is being driven by the fact that, for many companies, the benefits of using your product are often secondary to how people's connection to you makes them feel.

This theory was proven by runaway beauty product success Frank Body, which raked in $20 million in its first year by forming relationships with customers on Instagram. Talking to Foundr, the Frank body team of Bree Johnson, Erika Geraerts and Jess Hatzis shared their secret.

"We noticed a real niche with beauty and health brands on Instagram. It was the most influential market, but beauty companies were still speaking at a high level and not connecting with their customers. We saw young female users, who were quite impressionable, building an idea of themselves and who they were via the products they were purchasing and the brands they were engaging with. They also used social media really casually and conversationally every day, so we knew we had to talk in that way to them.

For us, social media was always just about having conversations, chatting to people and building personal relationships. We encourage founders to work out what their voice is for their product or service, and just really own it, and make sure their customers relate to it."

Jess Hatzis · Bree Johnson · Erika Geraerts

It's a sentiment echoed by famed musician and author Amanda Palmer, who has made a career out of connecting deeply with her fans—including asking them for help when she needed it. Back in the early days of crowdfunding, Palmer famously raised over $1 million on Kickstarter to produce an album, which led to her wildly popular TED Talk, The Art of Asking, and later her book of the same name.

Palmer sees community as the real linchpin of her success, and encourages founders to be authentic if they want to achieve long-term, people-powered success:

"The overarching rule is to communicate authentically, and try to build trust and keep it over time. A lot of companies get this wrong. They think an authoritative voice is believable and miss the fact that a human voice is so much more desirable. There's a real gold in being authentically human. Over the last 10 years, people are starting to understand this, and are peeling away the curtain of corporate bullshitty-ness and just saying, 'Hi, this is who we are.' By doing this you endear yourself to people, because people like honesty."

ASSEMBLING A TRIBE

Developing a robust following of people loyal to your brand is a massive marketing power play. Having a tribe at your back is a proven momentum builder for startups, but it needs to be tempered with the right balance of giving and asking. This means knowing when to add value and when to go in for the hard sell.

Tom Bilyeu and his Quest Nutrition co-founders understood the power of community in the early days of their brand, and focused their marketing efforts heavily in this area. As with content marketing, Bilyeu said community building should also be done with the right intentions—to offer people something that is going to truly add value to their lives.

"When people are building a community, it's about a real sense of service to that community. People are trying to do something awesome and we really wanted to help them do that. We were doing what we call mirror marketing, so we didn't want people to see us when they looked at Quest, we wanted them to see themselves. So it's always been a celebration of the fans, which gave them reason to tell their friends."

Bilyeu explained how Quest gave product away "hand over fist" in the early days, encouraging their target market to tell people if they liked or disliked it. Even when the reviews were negative, people appreciated their honest approach, and this became a major factor in the way the brand exploded.

"Not trying to steer people's comments gave us a pretty great recommendation. Some people didn't like it, and said so, but the vast majority loved it, and were grateful that we had showed an understanding of who they were, and what they were trying to do, that they just spread the word. The speed with which it caught on fire really, really caught us by surprise."

tom **bilyeu**

Online giant The Next Web has experienced the power of community as well, having grown a blog related to their annual tech conference into one of the web's largest media companies, now pulling in 8 million visitors a month. Co-founder and CEO Boris Veldhuijzen van Zanten told Foundr he believes that community should be a central piece to every startup business model. "We think it's an interesting way to look at the future of media companies. Everybody is looking for the business model, and the business model really is that you have a community."

If you are fortunate enough to have a community to serve, then you will always do better than the person that just has ideas. **I'm a big follower of the concept that a rising tide raises all boats.** Every dollar I've made has community attached to it.

chris brogan

Bestselling Author,
Owner Media Group CEO

Shaun Neff on Building a Great Brand

Work out what you stand for.

Gauge what the key factor driving your consumer is, and then break it down so you can figure out what will drive them to buy your product over someone else's.

Work extremely hard to convince them.

Be different and be relevant.
Keep it unique.

Nail three important attributes on every campaign: a great product, a great marketing story, and a great ambassador.

Melanie Perkins Started Small by Design

Featured in
Issue 38 -
*How Melanie
Perkins of
Canva is
Democratizing
Design*

Founder
Melanie Perkins

● ● ●

Job
Co-founder and CEO of Canva

Success Story
Perkins went from college student to successful entrepreneur, offering design software that anyone could use. At last count, Canva had 12.7 million users.

What's in a niche?

In the startup world, "niche" means a very specific purpose, and finding the right one can make all the difference. That could mean solving a niche problem or connecting with a niche audience, but it's an important step on the way to becoming a successful company.

As Melanie Perkins puts it, "Start niche and then go wide."

Perkins is the co-founder and CEO of Canva, an easy-to-use online tool for anyone with an interest in graphic design. The purpose of Canva was to create a platform that gave non-designers the ability to create beautiful graphics without having to spend years taking design courses.

"There's a lot of different companies in the marketplace that do all sorts of different things. But the reason we created our company was because we saw a huge gap," Perkins says. "So people can go and spend quite some time learning professional design tools and they can create incredible graphics. But a lot of people won't be able to put something together quickly for a presentation, or social media, or a pitch deck."

It's a simple idea that has resonated with investors like Guy Kawasaki, Lars Rasmussen, Owen Wilson, and Woody Harrelson, just to name a few.

But before Canva even started to close that huge gap in the market, Perkins knew that she had to start small.

While it was clear to Perkins that her idea would have vast appeal, it would have been too difficult and costly to try to disrupt the whole design world from the get-go. She needed a niche market that she knew was underserved, and would use her product frequently and with enthusiasm.

The result was a company called Fusion Yearbooks, which still operates today, a cloud-based graphic design tool that allows schools to design their own yearbooks. But it was also the birth of Canva. ●●●

"If we tried to tackle online design for everything under the sun to start with, it would have been very, very difficult. But because we started with a very specific problem, in a specific geography, it meant that we were able to solve that problem effectively."

It also enabled her to give her idea the stress test it needed. It was an invaluable learning experience that gave Perkins and her team the knowledge they needed about what problems people were facing with graphic design.

A few years later, only after she felt confident she had learned everything she could from her Fusion Yearbooks experience, she launched Canva.

Today, Canva is the biggest thing to hit the graphic design world since colored pencils—it's used across 179 countries by everyone from small businesses to some of the biggest in the world.

Even as it's grown, Perkins is still expanding into new niche markets, recently launching Canva for Work, a paid variation for marketing professionals. "It's been growing like crazy."

No matter how big your vision may be, it's all about starting small. Find your niche, find the people who love what you do, and change their world first before you try to change everyone else's.

Greg Koch
Made a
Connection
Over Beer

Featured in
Issue 24 -
*A Little
Arrogance Took
Stone Brewing a
Long Way*

Founder
Greg Koch

Job
Executive Chairman of Stone Brewing

Success Story
When Koch and partner Steve Wagner started Stone in 1996, their bold, hoppy beers were not what the market was after. But unwavering dedication to their product built the company into one of the most beloved craft breweries in the world.

As the startup world has flourished, cutting through the noise so that your message gets heard can often feel like shouting into the void.

So it's more important than ever to create a real, tangible connection with your audience, and the only way to do that is to be as honest and as genuine as possible.

In the 20 years since Stone Brewing Co.'s beer first appeared on taps and shelves, its founders have eschewed traditional advertising in favor of creating a rock-solid connection with their devoted customers.

It's a strategy that's paid off greatly, considering they've grown around 50 percent every year since they first started and are now one of the largest craft breweries in the United States.

▼

It wasn't always such a hit, however. When they started, Greg Koch and co-founder Steve Wagner liked beers with big, bold flavors and a ton of character. But they were not popular among the general public.

"At the time, in 1996, if a lot of people thought our beer tasted good, that meant that we were brewing mediocre beer. Because that's what most people thought beer was supposed to taste like, was mediocre beer," Koch says.

He knew that his style of beer wasn't going to appeal to everyone. But he also knew that he didn't need everyone to like it. He just needed to connect with the people who did.

In fact, the label on their now beloved Arrogant Bastard Ale begins: "This is an aggressive beer. You probably won't like it. It is quite doubtful that you have the taste or sophistication to be able to appreciate an ale of this quality and depth."

It's a bold beer and a bold attitude that some might not like, but Koch didn't want those people as customers. His customers would appreciate the audacity of his beer and the message that accompanied it.

"If people like what we do, that's great. But I really want people who love what we do to really love what we do. I want them to be passionate about it." Early on, Koch focused on

communicating to his customers in as real and authentic a way as possible. They needed to get across their own passion for their product.

"We were the first brewery to put a lot of text on a bottle of beer, no one else did. We'd put paragraphs, literally paragraphs, on bottles of beer that went into our philosophical take on the world, and what the flavor profile they could expect was, and why we were doing things the way we were."

That meant fans of Stone were always kept in the loop about what their favorite brewery was doing, what was coming next and what to expect. It made them feel like they were part of the Stone journey, not just another customer.

Despite the fact that there are millions of different beers in the world, it's that connection with their customers that keeps Stone Brewing Co. going strong. They didn't attempt to create a brand that appeals to everyone, just the people who would connect to their sincere, if arrogant, attitude toward making beer.

Today, Stone is considered one of the best breweries around, even being voted as the "All Time Top Brewer on Planet Earth" by readers of *Beer Advocate.*

"It doesn't take much—it just takes people to be passionate about what you're doing so that they become loyal customers."

Steve Kamb
Assembled His Tribe

Featured in
Issue 36 -
*The Hero's
Journey of
Steve Kamb*

Founder
Steve Kamb

● ● ●

Job
Founder and Rebel Leader of Nerd Fitness

Success Story
Kamb turned his fitness blog into an online and in-person community of hundreds of thousands of devoted followers.

Having a tribe of loyal customers can be the difference between a failed project and a success story.

While your product might bring in customers, it's often the sense of community that makes them stay. Knowing that you can share your experiences with someone else who knows what you're going through is a powerful feeling that can cultivate a loyal and passionate following.

That's been the case for Steve Kamb, founder of Nerd Fitness, whose other, more important title is Rebel Leader.

The Rebellion is what the Nerd Fitness members collectively call themselves, and Kamb has spent countless hours building it into the thriving community it is today. It's translated into tremendous personal and financial reward.

As the name suggests, Nerd Fitness is for those who love all things pop culture, from sci-fi to board games, and also happen to be interested in getting into shape. Like any other subculture, the pool of people compelled by the subject were already out there—all they needed was a lightning rod to draw them together.

To make that happen, Kamb started out by creating an online forum attached to his site, but he needed to make sure there would be a critical mass for something bigger to take hold.

▼

"When I first started the forums at Nerd Fitness, I was terrified of launching them and having the equivalent of a party where one person shows up every 10 minutes, but because they don't see anybody there, they leave. I wanted the party to be rocking by the time they showed up."

In order to achieve that buzz, Kamb set out to find the right people for his community, inviting 15-20 members of Nerd Fitness to be beta testers for its new forum.

"From day one, I made sure to recruit the right type of people. I was proud and confident enough to turn down people who I thought were not a good fit. I wanted to recruit the right kind of people who would help me moderate and foster and grow the community too."

Those initial members enthusiastically began to start posting in the forums and became a part of something that they were passionate about creating. By the time he made the forums public, they were bustling, and new members felt much more compelled to stay.

The community quickly grew, and Kamb realized that in order for it to be successful, it needed to be something that could thrive without his presence.

"I just continually tried to go out of my way and say, 'Guys, this is your community, I'm just a small part of it. What else do you need? What software do we need to purchase? What sort of contest should we be running? How do you feel about the direction of this?' Really try to give ownership to everyone that was part of the community and give them a chance to have their voice heard."

By rewarding and promoting active members of his tribe into moderators, Kamb set in motion a flourishing community around his brand and became a bona fide influencer himself.

One other crucial element—while being welcoming and inclusive was important, so was being somewhat exclusive. To make sure the forums were always a positive experience for his members, Kamb has made it clear that the Rebellion isn't for everyone. His team of moderators enforce a strict set of shared values.

"When we created our list of rules—some of them are slightly more controversial than others—we let people know that if you don't line up with these 11 rules, that's okay, but this isn't the community for you."

Members of the Rebellion now number over 300,000 strong and it doesn't look to be slowing down anytime soon.

chapter 06

MONEY MATTERS

06 MONEY MATTERS

SALES

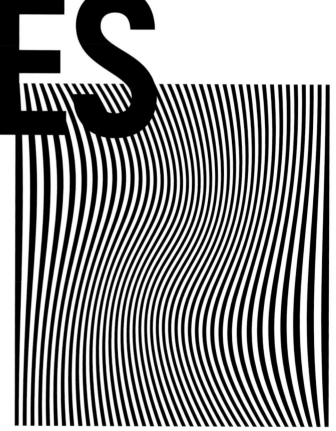

When you consider the degree of promotion required to get a business off the ground, it would be easy to assume that salesmanship is an intrinsic part of the entrepreneurial DNA. But the reverse is often true, according to celebrity investor Robert Herjavec. After watching thousands of budding entrepreneurs crash and burn during his tenure on *Shark Tank,* Herjavec discovered that most early-stage founders are in fact terrified at the prospect.

To become proficient at selling, Herjavec said, entrepreneurs first need to conquer that fear. Then it's a matter of giving yourself time to learn the ropes.

"Everything I've learned I've done wrong [first], learned from it, and done better next time. For me the hardest thing about sales was rejection. People say no to you a lot. You go through a phase when you think, 'Is it me?' when sometimes the product just doesn't fit, or it's not the right opportunity. But you've got to learn sales. Sales is everything in life. If you can't sell yourself, you're going to have a hard time getting ahead."

Effective selling is a matter of nailing three key attributes: **listening, qualifying, and knowing what motivates your audience, Herjavec said.**

"You gotta listen more than you talk. That's the big one. People don't want to be sold to today, they want to be educated. The other one is, before I teach you to sell, I have to teach you who to sell to. Always try to qualify who the right prospect is. The third one is motivation. You have to understand what motivates the other side, in anything. When people come on our show, they always tell us how good their business is, how it's going to make money, but they don't tell us how we're going to make money. You always have to understand what the other side wants out of it.

Robert
Herjavec

Not all entrepreneurs are as timid about sales as the *Shark Tank* contestants, however. Selling seems to have been encoded in Gary Tramer's DNA, for example. As a kid, Tramer and his friends would ride around on bikes stealing their neighbors' plants. The mischievous youngsters would then re-pot the plants into yogurt containers and sell them back to their original owners, using the money to load up on candy.

From these humble beginnings, Tramer has gone on to head up several successful sales-focused businesses, including popular website tool LeadChat. Along the way, he became something of a sales Jedi Master, and he shared with us plenty of gold on how to narrow down qualified leads. "There is a way of getting a 95 percent conversion rate—only speak to someone who you know will buy."

The first step, Tramer said, is to remove leads that are not a good fit for your product overall, before asking yourself three important questions: Are they a decision maker? Do they have the intention to buy, or are they just researching? Do they acknowledge that you can solve their pain point? Then, only spend your time reaching out to suitable leads. It requires persistence, especially when a lead has not responded to you after several attempts. "The amount of leads that we get through to and close on the sixth or seventh attempt is sometimes more than the first attempt."

Like Herjavec, Tramer also reminded founders to keep it real, believing people respond well to honesty, and someone who effectively tells the product's story.

"You are speaking to a person. People are hardwired mostly the same way. They don't want to be bullshitted. They don't want to be waffled around or coerced or manipulated. They just want to know what it is and how it's going to help them, and they want to be left to make the choice on their own. Be genuine; be a good storyteller."

Robert Herjavec's Five Sales Rules

1 Never forget the first thing you're selling is yourself.

2 Listen more than you talk. People want to be educated, not sold to.

3 Qualify. Know who to sell to.

4 Understand what motivates the other side.

5 Make it simple. Have your value proposition down to a few key points in 30 seconds.

06 MONEY MATTERS

Financial Literacy

As a startup founder, learning the numbers can be a make-or-break skill. It's another one that didn't always come as naturally to your entrepreneurial heroes as you might think. In fact, a resounding majority of Foundr interviewees have a tale to tell involving a failed past business, or an occasion where their current business was sailing perilously close to the edge.

Self-help expert Tony Robbins has recently undergone a directional shift, from motivating presidents and celebrities to educating the masses in all things finance. Robbins spent four years researching his book *Money: Master the Game,* meeting with more than 50 financial experts, including Warren Buffett and Carl Icahn. The book went on to hold the number one spot on the *New York Times* business bestseller list for several months in a row.

When it comes to money, Robbins stressed the importance of finding yourself a quality adviser.

"You need to get quality financial guidance. What I mean by that is, don't just get a damned CPA or an accountant. Most people don't even do that. Most of us entrepreneurs, we hate numbers, we hate accounting. Profit is a theory. I just want to warn every entrepreneur here. If you haven't already experienced this, you can have this huge profit, but at the end of the year, there's no cash!

"So accounting is a weird world, and you don't have to become an accountant, but you have to get somebody who can advise you. There are virtual CFOs now that you can get, and you can get somebody who can turn financial numbers into intelligence. You need someone to guide you, or you won't make it."

Daymond John learned the importance of mastering the numbers early on, but still much later than he needed to. In his early days, he lacked the financial intelligence to undertake even basic, but critical, activities like placing orders. After telling the story of how FUBU almost went bust on two separate occasions, John was quick to encourage founders to invest in their own financial knowhow. "The money is really a tool, and it can hurt you or help you."

Entrepreneurial expert Matthew Michalewicz similarly shared with us the importance of building your financial goals into your business early on, right alongside your deepest aspirations as an entrepreneur.

Financial smarts must go beyond your goals, however, including developing a realistic plan of how you intend to get there. Justin Dry and Andre Eikmeier, the crafty duo behind online wine giant Vinomofo, emphasized that getting your revenue model right should be a top priority. According to Eikmeier:

"What does financial success mean? Does it mean $10,000 a year? $100,000 a year? A million? Ten million? You begin by really thinking of these kind of things, and specific numbers in business terms, and then you begin planning and plotting your path to achieve those objectives. But all of them are in the context of your passion. That's how I've gone about it."

"There was always this faith that if we got the product right, the revenue model would work. It took us a while to really focus on the revenue model side of the business. It wasn't that we hadn't tried before—Vinomofo was just the first one that really took. That was the big learning: Get your revenue model right, and solid, and if you don't, have capital behind your business."

06 MONEY MATTERS
BOOTSTRAPPING

Along every entrepreneurial path, there's a set of choices that will profoundly shape a startup's direction. The question of whether to bootstrap or raise capital is one of those crossroads decisions.

Bootstrapping, aka when a company is started with little or no capital and is fueled by operating revenues or personal finances, is not a new idea in the business world. However, it has grown legs in recent years with the online economy opening up the door to a new breed of business owner.

For some founders, choosing to fly solo is a no-brainer. Others find it difficult to parse the pros and cons of each choice, and might wind up doing a hybrid of both. But if you do want to ride this journey by the strap of your boots, Foundr interviewees have dished up a ton of stellar advice.

For Julia and Kevin Hartz of Eventbrite fame, bootstrapping was decided by the fact that they simply wanted to get in and get started. To keep the company within its bootstrapped budget, the Eventbrite team turned to Lean Startup methodology without really knowing they were doing it. As Julia Hartz told Foundr:

"We were using our instincts, which were—we should be really scrappy and find people to start using this product right away. We didn't sit around and talk about things a lot. We just did. We built and we did and we iterated and we tested. We funded the company for the first two years and we actually got to break even."

julia hartz

As a serial entrepreneur who has been at the helm of several top tech companies, including Drip, Micropreneur, HitTail and DotNetNovice, Rob Walling is a bootstrapper through and through. Walling warns founders against getting caught up in the Silicon Valley myth that success is a reward reserved for billion-dollar companies with boatloads of funding. He patently rejects the theories that "the only businesses that matter are funded businesses," and that adding warm bodies is the best way to chart growth. "Headcount is not a bragging right...you don't need 50 people to run an eight-figure business, you can do it with 10 or 20."

rob
walling

As Walling sees it, there are no downsides to self-funding. Going it alone forces you to "build a real business instead of a dreamy unicorn goal." Too many entrepreneurs look at funding as permission to start. Launching is scary and waiting for funding becomes an easy excuse.

Another big fan of bootstrapping is Seth Godin. He literally wrote the book on it, *The Bootstrapper's Bible,* and he professes that you must absolutely nail the value you're offering to customers to make it work.

"The secret of starting a business with no money is to make a service or a product that your customers want so much that they will pay you for it in advance. The idea is, you go to a big corporation, and say, 'If I could do this, and save you $50,000, will you pay me $10,000?' And most of them, if they believe you, will say 'yes.' The key lies in identifying a problem, and having a scalable approach to solving it."

SETH **GODIN**

One word of caution when it comes to bootstrapping: starting a business without investors doesn't mean you can pull it off without cash. The level of cash you need will depend on your growth, but building a company demands it on some level, as Robert Herjavec attests.

ROBERT HERJAVEC

"It might be a line of credit or your credit cards, but cash is the lifeblood of your business. So if you're not going to raise capital, have a great relationship with your bank, in terms of line of credit. I think the only time you should bring an investor in is to help you grow faster."

Raising Capital

OK, now for the flipside. How do you bring in the big bucks when you need them? Whether you've had your heart set on pulling big investors in from day one, or your business has grown to the point where outside help is essential, there's plenty to learn before you go knocking down doors in Silicon Valley.

Ankur Nagpal, co-founder of online learning platform Teachable, ran a hugely successful app business during the early days of Facebook, all while he was still a teenager. When it came time to launch Teachable (then Fedora) a few years later, many people asked Nagpal why he went the fundraising route rather than putting his own money in. It's a question with a simple answer, Nagpal said, one that came down to the value he places on his own time, as well as a desire to bring other people into the fold. "I was already investing my most important asset into the business, so I didn't see the benefit in also investing my cash. What if it didn't work out? I also wanted other people invested in my success."

Nagpal said his experience disproves the assertion that startups relinquish control when taking investors on board:

"I'm always very impressed with bootstrap startups, but I feel that funded startups get a bad rap because of the way funding used to work. In the past, people would think, 'Why would you want to raise funding and lose control?' But if you look at term sheets available right now, you never actually give up control. We never gave up any operational rights to any investor, and we don't report to an investor. It's the best of both worlds. We have the capital to make mistakes—because ultimately that's what the value of capital is—but we still control our own destiny."

When it comes to actually rounding that capital up, Nagpal suggested going to AngelList and having them syndicate on your behalf.

"What was great about AngelList was that, instead of going to investors and getting rejected over and over, which did happen, people came to us, and so we got social proof really fast. That's one of my grievances with investing; it's driven so much by herd mentality. Many investors who didn't want a piece of us initially all wanted to come back after the angel listing went out."

After spending a decade building Y Combinator into one of the world's most influential startup incubators, Jessica Livingston has seen it all when it comes to capital raising. She spoke to a worrying trend she has observed among startups that have received first-round funding. They often take it for granted that a second round will be forthcoming. What this doesn't take into account, Livingston explained, is the fact that investors have much higher expectations the second time around.

"The average fund raise after YC is one to two million dollars. Fundraising is always hard, but for the most part, companies that seem promising are able to raise that amount of money. Then a year later they need more, and the founders think because they have done it before it shouldn't be a problem. They let the money in the bank dwindle down and then they get burned. Second time around investors want to see real growth and traction, backed up by evidence."

As easy as it is to back yourself into a corner and end up desperate for funding, one entrepreneurial champ touts the power of "No." For David Cancel, building and selling companies is a way of life. He has started and exited five companies over the past 16 years and is currently an adviser and investor to several more, including BigCommerce and Yieldbot. Cancel reminds founders that when it comes to courting investors, it doesn't hurt to play hard to get, explaining that his default answer to any investment offer or acquisition attempts is always no. So, how does he get companies to sell so quickly? "I try not to sell them. How do you get beautiful people to date you? Ignore them!"

06 MONEY MATTERS

Pitching

Whether you're pitching to investors, the media, or trying to attract top talent to your business, having an airtight pitch is absolutely key. And if shows like *Shark Tank* have taught us anything, it's that you only get one shot.

While parading your idea before a room full of blank-faced suits might sound daunting, the art of pitching can be distilled down into a few simple areas. You first need to understand what factors are driving each investor, and then build a narrative that connects with them on an emotional level. Your story should also be relatable; it should clearly outline the problem you are trying to solve, and demonstrate your passion.

Pitching and winning multimillion-dollar deals seems to be child's play for entrepreneur, investor and author, Oren Klaff. Founder of Intersection Capital and author of *Pitch Anything,* Klaff's approach is based on the little-known field of neurofinance. What he teaches is, therefore, not an abstract theory or reliant upon individual charisma. It's sequential, repeatable, and designed to hack the way our brains receive information. "The turning point was when I realized people want what they can't have. They chase that which moves away from them, and they only value that which they pay for."

That neediness is deal-making poison, he says. To mask the desperation that naturally comes with wanting another person to give you money, Klaff suggests you adopt a strategy called "prizing." This means flipping the frame to think of yourself as the prize to be won, instead of the money.

According to Klaff, success at pitching depends not on a physical product, but how well you can describe and solve a problem.

"The ability to raise money is not around introducing a solution or product, it's around having very, very sophisticated conversations around a problem. If you can define the problem well enough, then you can move into financing for a solution."

"So, my sense of it is 'Product, no product. Company, no company. Whatever.' You can raise more than a million dollars of financing to the degree you can describe a problem very, very well, deeply, from multiple angles: economically, socially, technologically, culturally, from a micro-view to a macro point of view; in terms of customer pain, in terms of market pain, in terms of competition. The better you can describe the problem, the more likely somebody is going to be excited about either your solution or any solution for a problem set."

Robert Herjavec had a similar take on pitching, encouraging founders to keep it simple and make sure they understand what potential investors are looking for. And if anyone knows what makes a good pitch, it's a guy who's sat through dozens of them on national television.

"People get bombarded with information all day long, they don't want big, complex stories. They want it to be simple. Have your value proposition down to a few key critical words you can say in 30 seconds or a minute. But also understand the motivation of the people you're pitching to. ... Everybody's gotta be on the same page. The mistake people make is, they try to bring an investor in, and that investor's goal isn't the same as theirs. They may want to grow the business and keep it for five years, and somebody else just wants to come in and make a quick return."

Herjavec also stressed the importance of self-presentation, when explaining how investors like himself, and his fellow *Shark Tank* investors, will always choose a convincing operator over a big idea.

"A great entrepreneur, who really believes in what they're doing, can make a so-so product great, and a bad entrepreneur can take even the best product and make it bad, can ruin it. We always say bet on the jockey not the horse. We usually make up our mind about somebody in the first few minutes.

"Everything that happens after that either supports that opinion, or something extraordinary has to happen for us to make us change our mind. So it's how people come out, how they speak, the cadence of their voice, how confident they are, and it all leads from there. If someone is really confident and humble, and they don't know their numbers, we're going to help them. If someone comes out who is cocky, or arrogant, and doesn't know their numbers— we hate them. We see that on the show all the time."

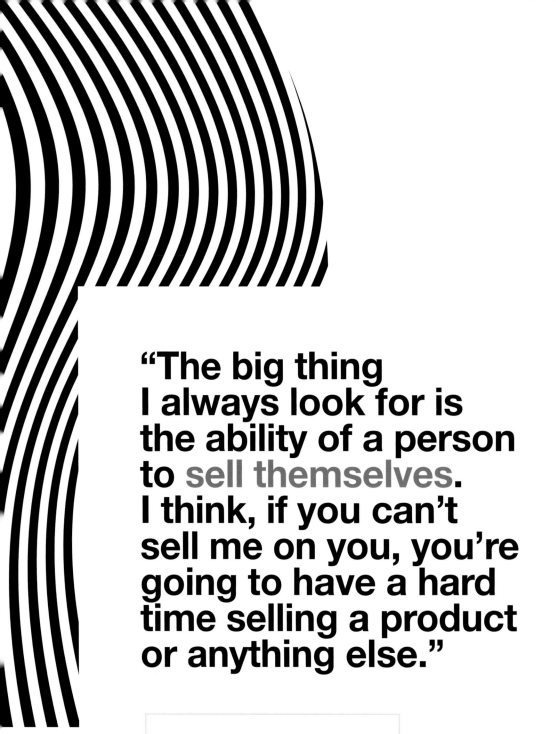

"The big thing I always look for is the ability of a person to sell themselves. I think, if you can't sell me on you, you're going to have a hard time selling a product or anything else."

Robert Herjavec
Author, Shark Tank Celebrity Investor

Present Opportunities, Not Ideas

Daniel Flynn is co-founder of Thankyou, a social enterprise brand of food and body products sold across Australia, with profits benefitting water, food, and health charities. But first, Flynn had to get his products into stores. He shared this advice on pitching:

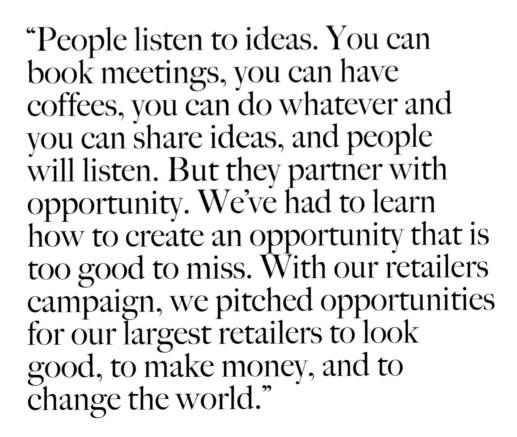

"People listen to ideas. You can book meetings, you can have coffees, you can do whatever and you can share ideas, and people will listen. But they partner with opportunity. We've had to learn how to create an opportunity that is too good to miss. With our retailers campaign, we pitched opportunities for our largest retailers to look good, to make money, and to change the world."

Equity split is always a tough topic between founders and investors. It's understandable that, as a founder, you want to protect your assets. However, there are other factors to take into consideration, like co-founder relationships and bringing in the resources your business needs to grow.

EQUITY

This is one area in particular where experts we spoke with had some varying opinions. For example, Robert Herjavec encouraged founders to retain their equity for as long as possible. "As an owner, and as a founder in your own business, your biggest payback is equity. Try to hang onto it as much as you can, for as long as you can."

However, as Jessica Livingston of Y Combinator sees it, reaching a fair agreement often means compromise. Livingston encouraged founders to split equity evenly whenever possible, explaining that over the course of a long journey, an equal partnership is fairer and less likely to cause friction.

"There may be one founder who came up with the idea and has been working on it for a year already. In that case, it's reasonable for them to bring in a co-founder with less equity. But you still need to have that conversation where you are both happy with the level of equity. I've seen many people agree to only 10 percent, versus the original founder getting 90 percent. Then when things progress, they think, 'I'm working just as hard, why do I only get the small amount?' You don't want that situation bubbling up when your company is doing well."

jessica livingston

Equity can be a hangup for existing partners, but it can also prevent great future partnerships from ever taking off. Award-winning ad man and startup adviser Alex Bogusky believes that bringing people on board with the necessary expertise is more important than any fears you might have over equity split.

When advising startups, Bogusky often sees people being too protective of their ownership stake, and as a result not bringing in the collaborators needed to make an idea valuable. Put bluntly, Bogusky suggested, "Don't choke this thing to death because you're so worried about what that percentage number is."

danae

CROWDFUNDING

These days, few ideas lie outside the bounds of what can be funded—you just need to convince people that your idea has merit. Crowdfunding gives ordinary people, including entrepreneurs, a door to financial backing that once stood closed.

Danae Ringelmann, **Indiegogo co-founder and chief development officer,** told Foundr that users of the platform have funded businesses, urban gardens, schools, medical cures, babies, films, and music tours (Babies? Yes, babies). When it comes to what makes a successful crowdfunding campaign, Ringelmann said there is one killer attribute.

06 MONEY MATTERS

"What makes an idea and a campaign successful on Indiegogo? There is one thing: it truly connects with an audience. Speak from the heart about what you're doing and why you're doing it and why you're the right person to be doing it. Be yourself."

Ringelmann explained that a great crowdfunding pitch is authentic, personal, and honest, without appearing too desperate:

"The biggest mistake I see people make is that, in raising money on Indiegogo, they ask for money. That's not what Indiegogo is about. Indiegogo is about bringing people together to ideate and create together, to make things happen together. Crowdfunding isn't a handout. It's a way to energize projects, flipping the switch from idea to reality, and making the world a better place."

danae ringelmann

It can be a lot more than just a funding mechanism, too. Musician Amanda Palmer crowdfunded $1.1 million, before sharing her story in a TED Talk that has garnered more than 8 million views. The experience elevated her celebrity in one way, but crowdfunding also served as an effective way to bring her closer to her fans, and to smash apart the impersonal, distant notion of celebrity.

"The TED Talk was about connecting the dots between my experience as a street performer and then as a musician asking for help. Having built a real connection in the community through the act of asking people for stuff, it obviously culminated in the successful Kickstarter. But there was also a resonance back to my life as a street performer, where you stand there and give your art away for free and hope that the sliver of humanity who wants to support you will be consistently generous as they pass. I know it works because I stood there for five years and did it."

amanda
palmer

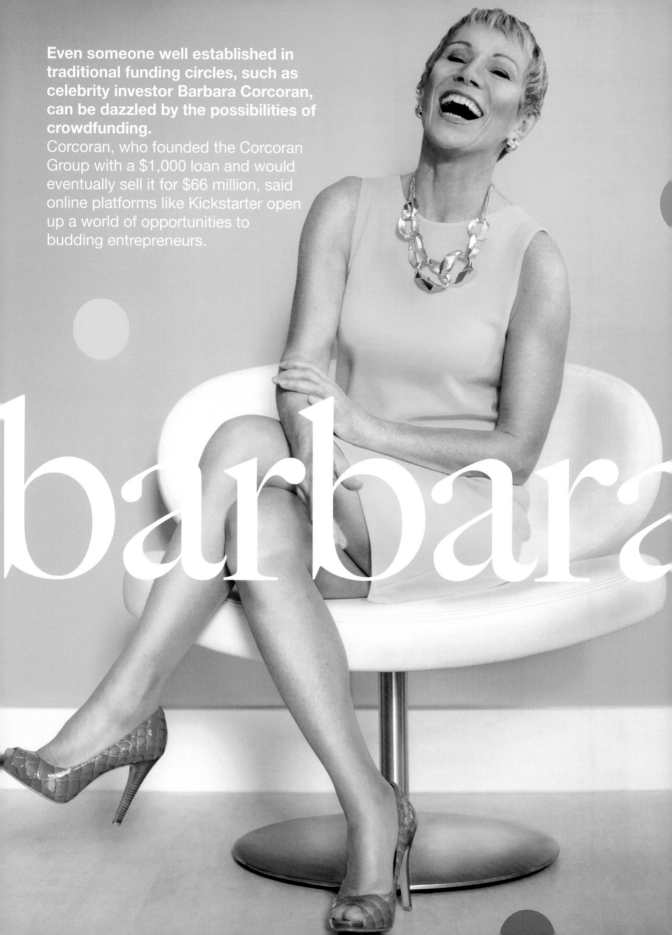

Even someone well established in traditional funding circles, such as celebrity investor Barbara Corcoran, can be dazzled by the possibilities of crowdfunding.

Corcoran, who founded the Corcoran Group with a $1,000 loan and would eventually sell it for $66 million, said online platforms like Kickstarter open up a world of opportunities to budding entrepreneurs.

barbara

"The access to capital isn't at your local bank — it's online. I would say that at least 40 percent of all the entrepreneurs we met on Shark Tank had already raised a lot of money online through crowdfunding. You can teach yourself how. Analyze successful campaigns. Figure out what works."

● ● ● **barbara** corcoran

06 MONEY MATTERS
SELLING

It's sacrilege to mention the mere idea of selling a business in front of some founders. For others, zeroes on a check have always been the endgame. But as a wise old crooner once sang, "You've got to know when to hold 'em, know when to fold 'em, know when to walk away, know when to run."

Pretty sage advice given the importance of timing when it comes to evaluating your business for sale or investment. Retailer Shaun Neff made sure the timing was perfect before selling off a chunk of his company to a private equity firm, as he told Foundr.

"In real estate, it's location, location, location. With a brand, it's timing, timing, timing. It's different for every business, but for me, I'm at the front of a very trend-driven business and culture that changes every day. So making an assessment involved looking at where Neff was at."

As Neff told it, triggering a sale starts with a company's profitability and includes a range of other factors that vary by industry. It's also important for your company to be in a strong growth position.

"No one wants to invest or buy something that is shrinking or dying. We're a very healthy, profitable company with a long-term brand, so for a new investor it was simple in the sense that we had a stable base and they could see where the brand was going to go."

Assuming the timing is right, and your business still has room to grow, let's say you're able to attract a buyer. But are you, personally, ready to hand it off to someone else? According to *Shark Tank* celebrity investor Robert Herjavec, there are three main reasons to consider selling your business: "If the money you are getting will change your life, if you think the market you're in has peaked, or if you don't want to do it anymore."

When referring to the 2000 sale of his first company, BRAK Systems, to AT&T Canada, **Herjavec** was happy to admit the decision to sell was a purely financial one.

"Back then we sold the business for $32 million, and I didn't have any money. I was putting everything I made into growing the business. We were always rich on paper, but poor in cash, like many entrepreneurs when they start out. Getting $32 million in cash was going to alter my life, and my kids' lives, forever. It was really hard. I always treated it like my baby, and I didn't want to sell it, but I'm really glad I did because it got me to where we are today."

CHRIS

DUCKER

06 MONEY MATTERS
OUTSOURCING

If there's one thing we've learned in our many conversations with entrepreneurs, it's that they are intensely passionate about their businesses. For this reason, some find it hard to hand over responsibilities to external parties, for fear they won't bring the right energy or quality to the table. But outsourcing the tasks you don't enjoy, aren't particularly good at, or are simply below your station as founder, can open up tremendous growth opportunities in your business.

Chris Ducker is CEO of Live2Sell group of companies, which includes a call center, a business to help people find virtual staff and a co-working space. Since kicking off with seven staff, Ducker has grown the global ranks of his team to include close to 300 employees.

Outsourcing is one of Ducker's most cherished concepts, so it's no surprise it lies at the heart of both his businesses, and his management style. In his view, outsourcing is, far and away, the best way for entrepreneurs to use their time effectively, as it frees you up to focus on activities with greater ROI. "Time is our most valuable commodity as business owners. As entrepreneurs, if we don't invest our time wisely, we're done."

The first step, Ducker said, is to ditch the idea that you need to do everything yourself, a misguided mentality he calls superhero syndrome. "Entrepreneurs, we have this misconception at first that we need to do everything ourselves. So even if we're not good at it, we'll still do it."

Ducker suggested that founders step away from this idea by developing three lists, which he calls the "3 Lists to Freedom" (see inset). Then, hire a virtual assistant (VA) to take over a range of caretaker duties, including basic email and social media. A competent VA can easily take care of online engagement, he says, and, if there are any queries they can't handle, they simply leave it for you to address when you are next online.

The impact of a VA is especially potent for handling email, "the bane of every entrepreneur's life right now." Ducker gets around 200 to 250 emails a day, but his VA has already replied to about 70 percent of them by the time he even logs on each morning.

landon
ray

For **Landon Ray**, co-founder and CEO of leading business automation platform ONTRAPORT, outsourcing allowed him and his co-founders to prioritize building a great culture, and making ONTRAPORT a highly-desirable place to work. It's a strategy that appears to have paid off—the company has been named one of *Fortune Magazine's* Best Small & Medium Size Companies to Work For, and one of the Achievers' 50 Most Engaged Workplaces. Not bad for three friends who spent their first two years in business working in a backyard yurt, with no heating or air conditioning.

"Once systems were in place, I was able to focus on providing a welcoming, engaging, supportive environment for our team members. I was no longer struggling to keep everything afloat myself; I had the time to look around and design a dream work environment for our ever-growing team."

This is a lesson that many entrepreneurs learn far too late in their careers, clinging to tasks to retain control, or in some cases because they just don't know what the alternatives are. That was the story for Gretta Rose van Riel, whose business took off before she learned the beauty of outsourcing. Van Riel told Foundr:

"[In the beginning] I was managing customer service, manufacturing, distribution—everything. I didn't know that there were third-party companies you could hire who could take the load off in certain areas. I'd never heard of drop shipping or experienced anything in e-commerce before. I just thought you had to take it all on yourself. Luckily, now I've learned better ways of managing things."

- Gretta Rose van Riel

"With modern e-commerce, everyone wants everything yesterday, so now we have a third-party logistics provider with consolidation centers in Melbourne, Hong Kong, the U.K. and U.S., which makes shipping a lot faster. Once you have everything systemized, it actually becomes a model, so we're able to use similar contacts for other products."

226

OUTSOURCE THIS !

Chris Ducker's **3 Lists to Freedom**

Things You **Hate Doing**

Things You Shouldn't Be Doing

To avoid getting bogged down with every little task, **Chris Ducker** suggests entrepreneurs prepare the following lists to determine which items can be outsourced.

Things You Can't Do Yourself

Chris Strode

Bootstrapped His Way to Success

Featured in
Issue 31 -
*The Big
Business of
Helping the
Little
Guys*

Founder
Chris Strode

● ● ●

Job
Founder and CPO of Invoice2go

Success Story
Strode hacked together invoicing software for small businesses during his daily train commute and other spare time. It has since grown from a one-person operation to a top-ranked business app.

It's an age-old entrepreneurial debate—bootstrapping versus seeking funding. Everyone has an opinion, but Chris Strode has experienced it from both sides. His advice: Bootstrap as long as you possibly can.

Strode is the founder and chief product officer of Invoice2go, one of the highest-grossing business apps on the market today, with more than 200,000 users.

Early in 2014, Invoice2go raised an impressive $35 million in its first round, valuing it at more than $100 million. But before Strode took a cent of funding, he had bootstrapped the multimillion-dollar company for *more than 12 years*.

In Strode's opinion, the only time a startup should seek funding is when it's looking to drastically scale, not when getting started.

When Strode first started Invoice2go in 2002, all he had going for him was an idea and a passion to build it. Instead of trying to land funding to hire a team, Strode decided to do it all himself. In fact, he didn't even hire the first employee until several years after the company launched.

Doing so meant working on his idea day and night, at every opportunity possible, all the while still working at his full-time job.

▼

"That was working in transit, back and forth on the train, working weekends, working Christmases, working Easter. So on top of doing a 40-hour job, I was probably doing another 60 hours on the app a week," Strode says.

While working 100 hours a week might not sound very appealing, it meant that Strode could keep overhead costs as low as possible by doing the product development himself. More importantly, it meant he had the freedom to be as flexible as he wanted and quickly pivot when necessary.

"I'm a big fan of lean startup methodology. That's pretty much how we built the company. Find out what worked and pivot, find out what worked again, and then pivot, and find out what worked, and you keep pivoting. That's the whole thing."

A natural side effect of bootstrapping that Strode recalled, is that it forces you to listen to your customer. Whereas bigger companies can throw money at marketing to try to make more sales, you don't have that luxury if you're bootstrapping.

If you don't have money to spend trying to convince people to purchase your product, your main focus shifts to building the best possible version of what you have to offer.

"The hardest time is figuring out what people want. I took a lot of functionality out of the app and that helped point people in the right direction. To make a hundred sales you need to have a really good understanding of what your customers want."

It was a valuable learning experience that taught Strode the true value behind his idea, who his target customers were, and the next steps he should take.

Strode pointed out an additional benefit of bootstrapping that comes into play if you do pursue outside funding:

"If you bootstrap and actually build a profitable company, you can just have a way better conversation when it comes to talking to VCs when you want to take it to the next level. Because you can continue to bootstrap, because you're profitable, you know the ball's in your court."

Rod Drury Raised Millions by Taking 'Baby Steps'

Featured in
Issue 27 -
*From Xero
to Hero*

Founder
Rod Drury

Job
CEO of Xero

Success Story
Drury's software accounting company, Xero, went public right from the start with a $15 million IPO in New Zealand, and has since raised several million more from prominent investors.

Whether you're looking for funds to start your business or to take it to the next level, courting investors is a daunting task.

Most venture capitalists and angel investors receive so many pitches, trying to find a way to stand out from the crowd is an uphill battle. Not only do you have to prove the validity of your idea, but you also have to prove that you're the kind of entrepreneur capable of bringing that idea into reality.

Rod Drury's current business Xero found success by doing things kind of backward. Very early on, Xero had a $15 million IPO on the New Zealand Stock Exchange. It's secured several million more from investors,

drawing heavyweight backers such as Craig Winkler and Peter Thiel.

The cloud-based accounting software company has reached more than 700,000 subscribers and more than $257 million in annualized committed monthly revenue. When it comes to the age-old question of when to raise capital, Drury has a simple answer:

"It's not a choice. It's what you can get. If you can raise capital then you should raise capital."

When it comes to raising such huge amounts, Drury attributes his success to his ability to clearly articulate his vision.

▼

"I think I've always been really good at telling the story and getting people to understand the scale of the story. I think being a clear-thinker, being able to communicate, and show passion and experience is key. It tends to be pretty binary, you either can do that or you can't," Drury says.

While it might seem completely obvious to you why your vision and your idea are going to create the next groundbreaking business, it isn't always so obvious to everyone else.

While investors can appreciate the passion you bring to the table, what they care about the most is whether or not your idea can turn into an actual working business. If you're not the person who can articulate that vision to investors, you need to find someone who can.

"The key thing is to have people on the team that can really explain to investors why it's such a good idea, and you've thought about the risk."

In all fairness though, Drury wasn't some unknown entrepreneur who managed to talk his way into millions in funding. By the time he started Xero, he was already a seasoned pro, with a strong track record as the founder of multiple successful startups.

For early-stage entrepreneurs, Drury recommends building their portfolios as soon as possible, even if it means bootstrapping.

"The first one you'll probably have to bootstrap, or ask friends and family, or take a loan, or have parents pay, to get the money in. But as you get more and more success, it gets easier to raise external money.

"For early entrepreneurs, I think you should treat entrepreneurship as a series of baby steps. With each one, you get a bit more capital, a bit more experience, your network builds, and you'll always find better ideas later anyway. It's more about getting into the game and giving your investors a good experience and it allows you to go bigger, bigger, and bigger."

It's important to remember that no matter how great your vision, most funded startups will fail, and most of all, investors are looking for a return.

That means the best way to appear attractive to investors isn't by dazzling them with an idea, but by showing how dependable you are as an entrepreneur. At the end of the day, investors are betting on the people behind the idea.

chapter 07

YOU AS FOUNDER

Leadership

Leadership is one of the toughest skills for entrepreneurs to master, both novice and veteran. It's something of a minefield, in terms of knowing how much you should learn by doing, and how much to dig out of books or courses.

There are certainly many different leadership styles outlined in popular theory. But regardless of which style comes most naturally to you, one thing is certain— becoming a quality leader requires you to do more than just stick a few choice quotes to the wall of your office.

As Darrell Wade sees it, great leadership starts with both offering and encouraging mutual respect. After three decades at the helm of group tours giant Intrepid Travel, Wade believes mutual respect is crucial if you want people to put their faith in you.

"A group of people need respect above everything else. If you have that, it's really easy to lead, because you can work things through, and that team will be reasonably happy deferring to you. You do it a few times and people get more and more respect for your style. You start to work well together because you're harnessing their brains in a constructive, forward-thinking way. Then it becomes a reinforcing, self-fulfilling prophecy because you're working with a group of people who have confidence, faith in themselves, and faith in you as a leader. But really, it's an internally built faith that starts to propagate the future, and it works."

Respect certainly can go a long way, but leadership also requires proactive planning. It's tempting to just sit at the helm once you've got a good team dynamic working, but things constantly evolve. For AOL Co-founder Steve Case, strong leadership requires you to effectively anticipate the future, and remove any roadblocks so the path ahead for employees is clear.

"You have to keep adjusting and understanding what the next challenge is. It was always helpful for me, in those early days, to look even a year down the road and try to position now for that future that was imminent. To not just be behind the eight ball, trying to play catch up. Particularly as we were starting to accelerate our growth, just trying to understand what kind of organizational structure we might need a year down the road, and putting that in place before we needed it, not after."

Then again, sometimes the roadblock standing in the way of your team is you. Fellow billion-dollar startup founder Rod Drury of Xero further believes that once the way forward is set, a good leader should also know when to stand aside.

"It's my job to say yes because, as you get big, corporates want to say no. So I think 'How can I say yes to things?' to encourage people to think big, to take ownership and run as fast as they can. I'm always trying to unblock things and keep the urgency up as much as I can. This is why I tend to bounce around the business— because I've got such great people running it, it frees me up from being too prescriptive about my day."

Embracing a leadership style that gives your team a lot of slack can also go a long way toward maintaining your own sanity. This gets back to those priceless principles of trust and delegation, two things that Ankur Nagpal of Teachable champions. He's even got it down to something of a formula.

"What I tell people in the first few days, is, 'I'm hiring you because I think you're very smart, and because I want you to reduce the number of decisions I have to make. Part of your job is making decisions on my behalf, and in return, I'm going to allow you to make the wrong decision 20 to 25 percent of the time—as long as most of your decisions are correct. I think this has been massively helpful. Initially it's hard to do, but you need to find smart people, empower them, and be good to them."

SUCCESS

If you type the phrase "how to become a successful entrepreneur" into Google, it will come back with thousands upon thousands of opinion pieces detailing the top 10, 15, 75 most important things you must do to make it to the top.

But what is success? What does it mean for you, or for entrepreneurs in general? Or, in other words, how long is a piece of string?

Foundr interviewees have had much to say on the subject of success, beginning with none other than The Huffington Post co-founder Arianna Huffington. It's not a stretch to say Huffington is one of the titans of the digital media world, gracing the *Forbes* World's Most Powerful Women list in 2013, and the *TIME* 100 list in 2006 and 2011. After a stress-and-fatigue-related fall caused her to reevaluate her priorities, Huffington published the book *Thrive* in 2014. Since then, she has championed the idea that society needs to redefine what it means to be successful.

Huffington had a knack for visualizing long-term goals from a young age—goals that were often deeply tied to both power and money. In *Thrive*, Huffington details how society's mad drive for these two goals is now so unhealthy, it's making people sick to the point of even being fatal. The idea that power and money define success is inherently wrong, Huffington said.

"So many of us have opted to live in a way that's fundamentally unhealthy and unfulfilling because, as a society, we have been operating under the collective delusion that burning out is the necessary price for accomplishment and success. Recent scientific findings make it clear that this couldn't be less true. Not only is there no tradeoff between living a well-rounded life and high performance, performance is actually improved when our lives include time for renewal, wisdom, wonder, and giving."

● ● ● **arianna** huffington

While healthy balance is a crucial factor in finding success, that doesn't mean having a lack of intensity, according to a number of entrepreneurs we've spoken with. *Shark Tank* celebrity investor Barbara Corcoran said successful founders need to have a certain amount of killer instinct. "If you're not competitive, you're not going to succeed in building a business."

Just as in any competition, resilience is key. The ability to lose, dust yourself off, and get back in the game is a common trait she sees in successful business owners. "It's their ability to take a hit. Their ability to take a hit and not feel sorry for themselves," Corcoran said.

Another big part of winning the game, as Corcoran sees it, is playing to your strengths, which gives an entrepreneur a competitive edge, but also illuminates which business ideas hold promise. If you know what you're good at, you can eliminate nonstarters.

"The first thing I do is I try to figure out what the individual entrepreneur's strengths and weaknesses are. What are they good at? What are they bad at? (An idea) has to suit the entrepreneur or it ain't going to go nowhere."

That being said, success in business isn't nearly as clear-cut as, say, winning a basketball game. There's no buzzer, no scoreboard, no league standings. So how do you know when you're there?

Robert Greene is the world-renowned author of five bestselling books on power and seduction, including *The 48 Laws of Power*, which has sold over 1.2 million copies worldwide. Greene discouraged founders from viewing success as an endpoint, but rather a journey that should be enjoyed. "If you're someone who is only focused on the end result, which is money, power, fame, you won't have the patience to get there. You have to enjoy the process itself."

The reason enjoying the process is so important is that success takes a long time to achieve, Greene said. There are no shortcuts. Becoming a master of your field takes years of dedicated commitment and practice. In other words, if you think you can learn how to play the guitar or speak Cantonese just because you have an app for it, think again.

"I am a little concerned with people in the digital age believing that, because our technology is so powerful, they can do anything. I want to combat the mental disease that is spreading across the planet that things can come easily and quickly. Mastery is eminently attainable by anybody, if you go through the process. It leads to something that is a lot more fulfilling. It's not just a boring 10,000-hour trudge to learn something. It's the most exciting adventure you could be on."

Robert Greene

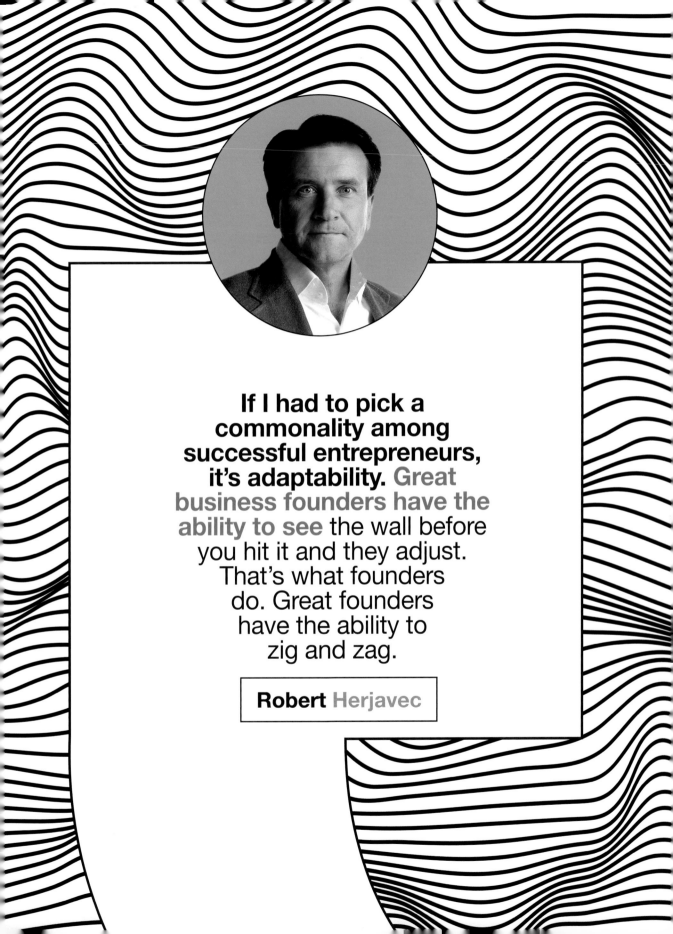

If I had to pick a commonality among successful entrepreneurs, it's adaptability. Great business founders have the ability to see the wall before you hit it and they adjust. That's what founders do. Great founders have the ability to zig and zag.

Robert Herjavec

07
PRODUCTIVITY

As an entrepreneur, there are almost never enough hours in the day. So when time is your most valuable commodity, managing it skillfully can become your most powerful weapon. Time management is so valuable, in fact, there are almost as many touted productivity hacks and tools on the internet as there are cat videos. But when it comes to developing productive practices, Foundr interviewees have offered a ton of wisdom.

Tim Ferriss has been one of the world's most prominent and respected experts when it comes to escaping the trap of endless work hours. He challenged the world to rethink its approach to work in the seminal startup and productivity book *The 4-Hour Workweek*. When telling Foundr of an early experience with some time-consuming suppliers, Ferriss said being productive also means being able to identify time-wasters:

"People put up with a lot when they are a startup—and sometimes you have to. But there are going to be people who make it their full-time job to complain. That's just a matter of statistics. If you have enough customers, you are going to have one or two out of every hundred who have nothing better to do than to make you their full-time priority. And it's helpful to choose, in advance, what your policies are in terms of dealing with that."

"In my case, I got to a point where I was having trouble sleeping, I was losing self-respect because I had a number of wholesalers who were browbeating me. And I took it for a long period of time until I decided one day, enough is enough. I am focusing on the wrong people. When I spend hours or days trying to fix an imaginary problem for this customer, that prevents me from trying to replicate my lowest maintenance, highest profit customers."

By taking charge and showing leadership—Ferriss sent an email to the troublesome parties, which clearly outlined his policies and politely gave people the opportunity to take their business elsewhere—he nullified the issue and gained back his time.

"All of a sudden the power dynamic shifted— they realized, 'If I don't have this product I'll lose all this profit margin because the product is selling really well.' It completed flipped it on its head and they were all on best behavior. I was immediately sleeping better and having better quality relationships."

**Rod
Drury**

High-maintenance business relations are only the beginning when it comes to the black holes that can suck up an entrepreneur's time. We all see it slipping away, whether to conference calls, meetings, iPhone apps, Netflix, pick your poison. CEO of Owner Media Group, Chris Brogan, called this out, believing people would have more time to get things done if they simply stopped wasting it.

"The way you do it, is you cut out all the baloney in life. I mean, there's just so much silliness. For instance, I try to make any interviews 20 minutes or less. If I have to have a meeting, if I'm forced to have a meeting, I do it as brief as possible. I don't watch too much television. There's a lot of things you can cut out of your life before you tell me you don't have enough time."

Rod Drury also knows a thing or two about the kind of productivity habits required to run a wildly successful business. He is, after all, co-founder and CEO of a company that went public on day one, raising $15 million out of the gate with only 100 customers. As Drury told it, productivity is not simply about your own output, but also your ability to create a sense of urgency among those around you.

"The biggest thing I've learned in business is actually making things happen. Picking up the phone and asking why. Why aren't we doing it now, why is it going to take a week? Let's go and do it today. Just driving urgency, and getting things done, puts you so far ahead of most other businesses that you can win in a really significant way."

The Hustle

If there's one trait that we see most often, and hear about the most, that sets entrepreneurs apart from the rest of the population, it's the level of effort they invest in their projects. Call it hustle. It just takes a special kind of person to show up, day after day, through all the knocks and bumps, and commit to getting the job done.

It's certainly not a matter of luck, or even hacks, as renowned entrepreneurial personality Gary Vaynerchuk put it. You make your own luck and nothing does it like cold, hard hustle. "My hustle is better than everybody else's, so I have to bet on it. I bet on my strengths."

A staunch advocate of simple hard work, Vaynerchuk has built a multimillion-dollar empire on the back of his ball-of-fire personality. From where he sits, hustle even wins the day over talent.

"I'm probably equally talented to a lot of people out there. I think I have a lot of talent, but I think a lot of people do. What I'm completely convinced of is that I don't think people can outwork me."

Again, we hear this a lot, and we're sorry to say that so many people who have faltered out of the gate simply don't want to put in the hours. Those who started strong and have been around for decades are almost always the relentlessly hard workers. Guy Kawasaki is one of those entrepreneurial legends, and says his willingness to "grind it out" has set him apart from his peers all his life.

"I'm willing to work hard. I can outwork most people. There are people who are smarter than me, and there are people who can work harder, but there are very few people who are smarter and can work harder."

Another icon who got his start in the early days of Silicon Valley, Steve Blank, had a very similar take, noting that it's those who are eager, the go-getters, who outpace the rest. Showing up, day after day, is 80 percent of the game, he said.

Continuing this streak of bad news for the brilliant slackers out there is Jessica Livingston. She's observed a steady stream of founders over 10 years at YC—including the brains behind Airbnb, Reddit, Dropbox, Instacart, Scribd, and Weebly—and has identified the sheer will to succeed as the thing that separates the wheat from the chaff:

● ● ●

"A good chunk of entrepreneurship is showing up. You could be a genius, you could have insight, but if you're not standing there volunteering for stuff that interests you, and showing up a lot—for both the good jobs and the bad—you're not going to get picked for the team. So while there are a lot of other parts to entrepreneurship, it doesn't get handed to you. It's not assigned. It's for those who stand up and take a leap. That was the story of almost everything I did."

steve blank

"When we first started Y Combinator, we thought if someone is a really good programmer that will translate into them being a really good founder. But that's not true. It's determination. How much you can persevere through all the problems you're going to have, and keep pushing forward."

I don't care about your passion, and I don't care about your idea. Those are myths that hold us back. What you need is thirst.

Seth Godin
Entrepreneur, Author,
Squidoo.com Founder

07 YOU AS FOUNDER

Relationships

If you've signed up for the life of an entrepreneur, there will more than likely be a string of long, at times very solitary, days and nights ahead of you. But that doesn't mean you can get by with your only relationship being the one you maintain with your business.

To the contrary, relationship and self-help expert Tony Robbins believes your long-term business success is wrapped up in the quality of your relationships:

"Your relationships are critical. I've dealt with so many people over the years, billionaires, who had all the money in the world but their relationships were horrible, and they're miserable, because the quality of your life really is based on relationships."

A similar principle applies to the way you interact with your business partners. Jessica Livingston drew a parallel between these important partnerships and marriage. After seeing countless founder relationships sour, Livingston told Foundr that aligning your goals and having regular, honest conversations goes a long way towards maintaining healthy co-founder relationships. One of the reasons partnerships do fail, Livingston said, is the fact that these relationships are often manufactured.

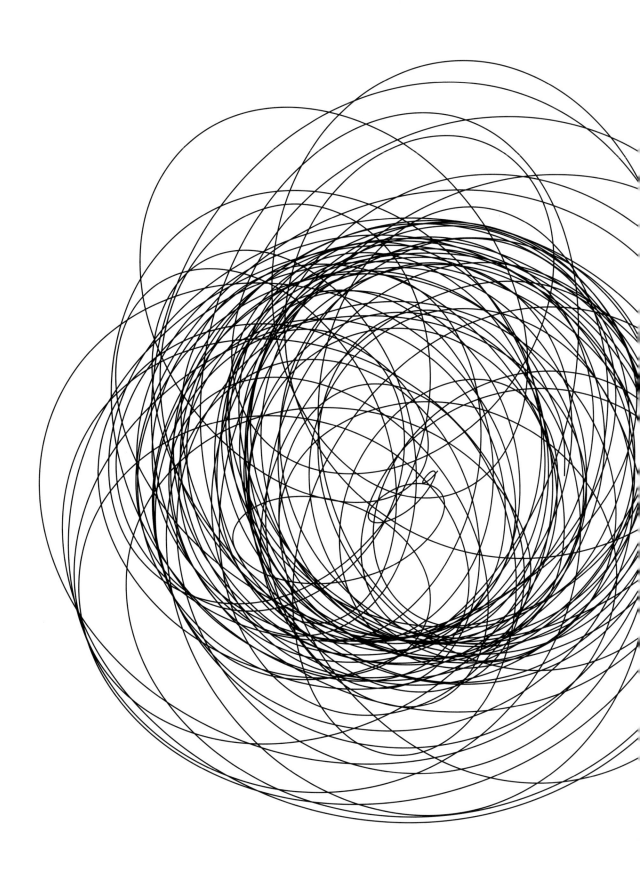

"These days, founders get started together less organically than 10 years ago. A founder might want to start a company but they don't have a programmer, so they bring in someone they have no history with. It's not really surprising if they don't get along. I have seen many founders break up because they don't have experience working together, or because they have different work ethics or goals."

Livingston went on to suggest practical pieces of advice for anyone considering working with a person they don't know very well. First, test the waters on an informal project, she says. Working together for even one month will give you a sense of how well you collaborate. Then, have a lengthy conversation about what your endgame is—a quick money spinner, or an in-it-for-the-long-haul adventure.

Similar values and goals aren't quite enough to cut it, however. You need to nail the right mix of talents and skillsets to build an enduring partnership, according to **Quest Nutrition's** TOM BILYEU.

"I would be nowhere without my two partners. You need somebody **who can** dream, and you need somebody who can **paint a vision**, **no question.** But you also need somebody who can watch your financials and execute on that incredibly well. If we hadn't had my business partner, Mike, who just focuses relentlessly on the finances, we would never have been able to get where we are now."

Jessica Livingston's Co-Founder Relationship Tips

1 **Communicate or perish**
Poor communication is one of the most common reasons founder relationships fail.

2 **Avoid financial squabbles**
Be crystal clear on your financial endgame. A quick sale, or are yo in it for the long haul?

Learning

As much of a drag as it can be working for big corporations, one thing they really have going for them is that the decent ones often provide valuable personal development opportunities. As an entrepreneur, however, most learning and development is done on the job.

Brain trainer to the stars Jim Kwik believes that, if knowledge is power, learning is your superpower. Everyone person can do it, he said, we just weren't taught how. That's right, we need to learn how to continue learning.

"In many ways, you were taught a lie, that your intelligence, your memories, your learning is fixed, like your shoe size. We know from the past few decades of brain science research that this is absolutely not true. We have an incredible capacity to learn, just not by consumption. We learn by creation, by rolling up our sleeves and getting involved."

Entrepreneurs especially should be using this to their advantage, by prioritizing simple learning activities.

"We live in a very competitive information age. It feels like we're trying to take a sip of water out of a fire hose. Knowledge is both power and profit. Entrepreneurs need to be committed to learning, and schedule time for it. Not for things like emails and project management, but to listen to a podcast or do 30 minutes of reading per day. Because if you're not feeding your mind, you're falling behind."

Ongoing improvement and learning is something that extends well beyond formal education, Robert Herjavec agreed. The *Shark Tank* investor explained how important it is to stay open to new information and ideas, no matter where you are in your career.

"I think I've always had a great ability to absorb knowledge. I have a lot of respect for people who love what they do and if I can learn from them. I don't have a very big ego when it comes to doing things better. If you're doing something better than I am, I am happy to take it from you and apply it to our business. So I learn from people all the time. I'm always a student of learning and success and what makes people tick."

Robert Herjavec

That need for curiosity and openness applies to daily business interactions, but entrepreneurs also need to proactively seek out new wisdom from their idols. Business guru **Matthew Michalewicz** encouraged founders to approach people they admire, where appropriate, and pick their brains for ideas and insights.

"Go and meet and spend time with people that are doing what you want to be doing, and are making money from it. If you can get access to them and have a cup of coffee and ask the question, how did you get here? How can I do what you're currently doing? Because those conversations are your market research."

MATTHEW MICHALEWICZ

" You want to learn faster? Be curious, and fascinated, like children."

Jim Kwik

BRAIN & LEARNING EXPERT,
SUPERHERO YOU FOUNDER

CRITICISM

Every idea has
it detractors,
as do those who
dream them up.
From investors
telling you your
idea sucks,
to family and
friends
who mock
your dream,
entrepreneurs
can come up
against
a fair amount
of flak.

As Dave Goldberg once told Foundr:

"You learn from hearing people's opinions, but you also learn from debating some of that stuff with them, too. It's not okay to ignore people when they tell you it's not going to work out, and they have good reasons why—you need to listen to those reasons. **You need to be able to explain to them why they're** wrong."

As helpful as it can be to engage with your critics, it's also important to not fall prey to an overabundance of advice. The Next Web's Boris Veldhuijzen van Zanten noted that this is especially true, given that there are so many different areas of business and the landscape is changing constantly. At some point, there's value in just following your nose.

> My advice is, don't listen to advice too much, and follow your own heart. We started our company. We were ambitious and we had dreams and a vision of what it could be. But mostly we went with the flow. We looked at the opportunity, and we listened to our audience to see what problems they had and what solutions we could offer. This is different for every industry and every time."

Boris Veldhuijzen van Zanten

MARIE
FORLEO

His sentiments were echoed by TV host and motivational speaker **Marie Forleo,** who believes successful entrepreneurs know when to trust their gut. In Forleo's opinion, early-stage entrepreneurs should be encouraged to make their own decisions, and not be too easily swayed by what the experts, or the industry, are saying.

If it doesn't feel right for you, for whatever reason, you've got to listen to that. People who are truly successful, that's what they're able to do. **They're able to listen** to their own instincts outside of the noise, and they're able to go in a different **direction** and not self-doubt **when they do.**

07 YOU AS FOUNDER

ADVERSITY

Everyone faces obstacles, both professionally and personally; it's part of this thing called life. Entrepreneurs, however, can expect more ups and downs than the average Joe. Mental toughness in the face of adversity becomes critically important. You might have incredible marketing chops, off-the-charts productivity skills, and be wildly passionate about your business. But without mental toughness, you'll struggle to stick it out when the going gets tough.

You can take heart, however, from the fact that many high-profile entrepreneurs also got their education from the School of Hard Knocks.

As entrepreneur and author Steve Blank explained, failures in the entrepreneurial world are like battle scars. In Silicon Valley, calling someone a failed entrepreneur is another term for experienced. "In Silicon Valley, you're not considered a failure if you blow 35 million dollars, or fifty, or a hundred. You're considered someone who learned a lot and is probably worth investing in again."

Martin Hosking can certainly relate to this, as his early startup collapsed amid the late 1990s tech bubble bursting. He's now back on top as CEO of Redbubble, but was quick to point out that on some level, being an entrepreneur simply means accepting that you're going to make mistakes.

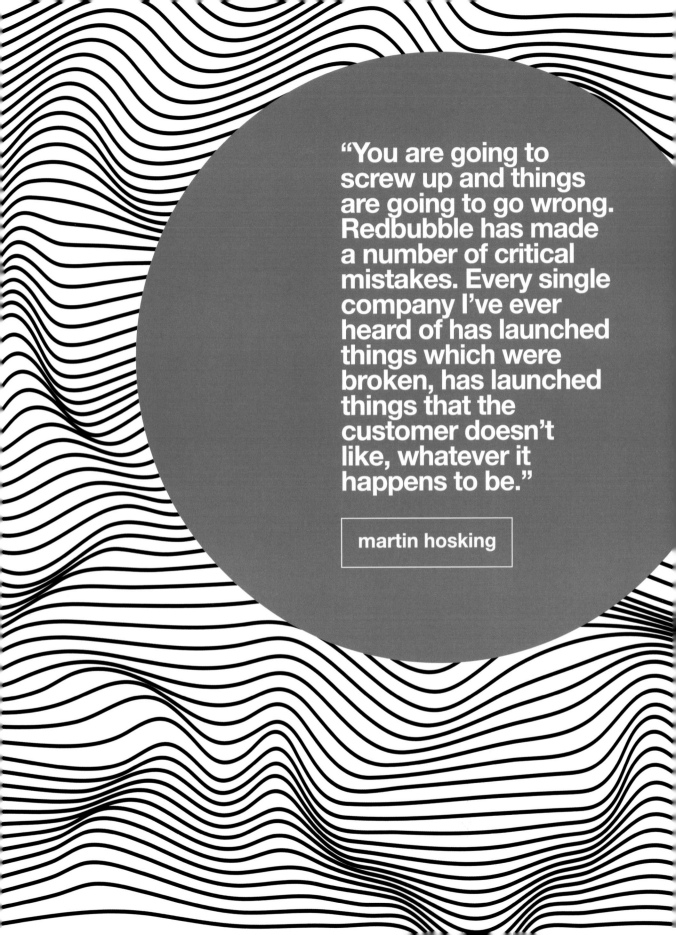

"You are going to screw up and things are going to go wrong. Redbubble has made a number of critical mistakes. Every single company I've ever heard of has launched things which were broken, has launched things that the customer doesn't like, whatever it happens to be."

martin hosking

Researcher and author Brené Brown is a thought leader on the subject of human connection. Through her work, and famous TEDx Talk on The Power of Vulnerability, Brown takes a refreshing, data-based look at life and success. In the entrepreneurial community, one dominated by masculine values and "tough-guy" attitudes, Brown breaks through the noise with her message to accept and even embrace discomfort.

brené brown

"Entrepreneurship is vulnerable by definition. If you are not experiencing uncertainty, risk and emotional exposure, you are not an entrepreneur. I don't want to work with an entrepreneur who puts on a brave face. I want to work with an entrepreneur who is actually courageous. I believe in truly brave people. That means being vulnerable and asking for help and admitting when they went wrong. We don't need brave faces running business. We need brave people."

Speaking of tough guys, even some of the toughest around have suffered blow after blow, and come out all the better for it. Celebrity brain trainer Jim Kwik knows that struggle is something we all experience, even for his celebrity pals **Sylvester Stallone** and **Arnold Schwarzenegger.**

"I always think genius leaves clues. What does it take to be a champion? Arnold told me it's all about pushing through the pain. Sylvester said, ask yourself if the pleasure will be worth the pain. The theme is, inevitably you're going to have struggles, but if you allow them to, they can become your strengths and can also become the way you serve others."

brene
brown

Tony Robbins is another larger-than-life figure who probably seems invulnerable to the slings and arrows life throws at us. But, in fact, it was Robbins' childhood experience of witnessing his parents' bankruptcy that shaped his will to succeed, he told Foundr. It's all a matter of shifting your energy and turning pain into gain.

"That hunger, you either get it because you've had enough pain and instead of letting the pain destroy you, you turned it into drive; or you get that **hunger** because you get inspired by something larger than yourself, or get around people that are hungry and let them impact you. I always tell people—the source of energy is not you. The **source of energy is a mission bigger than you,** if you can find something that **you're excited** about."

Adversity can do more than build strength. It can also send you in new, unexpected directions as you dodge, weave, and recover. When encouraging founders to persevere through the hard times, **STEVE CASE** referenced the early days of AOL, during which he and a small team of employees toiled away for almost 10 years, before their dream of providing mainstream internet access came to fruition.

"Recognize and remember that revolutions often happen in more evolutionary ways, which is why perseverance is so important. It was a challenge for us to get people to believe, and initial interest in the company was pretty modest. But, over time, people got it, and it started to grow more rapidly. But it was a circuitous adventure, it wasn't a straight line. There were a number of times when we thought we weren't going to survive. But, thankfully, we stuck with it, we persevered and figured out some new angle, some new direction or twist, and eventually we were able to continue moving forward."

Business is a series of linked recoveries that you later elegantly describe as a plan.

Hap Klopp
Former CEO,
The North Face

07 YOU AS FOUNDER
WELLBEING

We've heard it a thousand times: avoiding extreme stress, keeping fit, and eating well are the keys to a long and healthy life. We get it (and we don't need a bronzed Adonis with washboard abs to keep reinforcing the message).

However, the importance of health and wellbeing does become a little more urgent when you're a gut-busting entrepreneur, juggling a mountain of pressures, responsibilities, and expectations. We have a tendency to put everything after the business, including our physical and mental health, and it takes a serious toll, fast.

Amid the noise of modern life, mindfulness—focusing on the present, while calmly acknowledging and accepting your emotions as they arise— often achieved through meditation, is a simple and powerful way to combat stress, in addition to boosting self-awareness and productivity. So many wildly successful people meditate, from Richard Branson to Tim Ferriss, that it's become increasingly difficult to shrug off.

Andy Puddicombe, one of the minds behind meditation app success story Headspace, told us that daily practice is the best way to step away from the relentless cycle of thought that is synonymous with running a business, and start cultivating a sense of calm and clarity.

"I've never met anyone in the world who wouldn't like to feel a bit less stressed. It's universal, part of the human condition. Our minds are overactive. They are overstimulated, and I think, nowadays, the mind is so overstimulated that we don't even know how to stop it."

Puddicombe went on to explain that, whatever your motivation for undertaking meditation or mindfulness practice—be it for overall well-being, or because you want to be more focused or clearer in your decision-making— one of the greatest overall benefits is actually improved relationships.

"If we don't have a healthy relationship with ourselves internally, if we're always berating ourselves and giving ourselves a hard time, that is inevitably our experience of relating to others as well. There's a direct reflection. So unless we train ourselves, it's really hard to have healthy relationships with others. When you think about what that means in the workplace, and in startups and collaborative teams where you're working so closely together, when everyone is meditating, in my experience, it just takes the whole thing to another level. It just makes everything so much quicker."

ANDY PUDDICOMBE

arianna

According to digital media mogul Arianna **Huffington,** switching off is another high-value wellbeing activity that's easy to incorporate into your daily routine. In today's hyper-connected world, Huffington said disconnecting from the devices that have enslaved us is becoming more and more essential.

"The first stages of the internet were about data and more data. But now we have plenty of data—indeed, we're drowning in it—and all the distraction we could ever hope for. Technology has been very good at giving us what we want, but not always what we need. Wherever we look around the world, we see smart leaders, in politics, in business, in media, making terrible decisions. What they're lacking is not IQ, but wisdom. Which is no surprise; it has never been harder to tap into our inner wisdom, because in order to do so, we have to disconnect from all our omnipresent devices—our gadgets, our screens, our social media—and reconnect with ourselves."

arianna huffington

Indeed, so many of today's entrepreners devote their lives to improving the world using technology and our precious devices. But you would be surprised how many of them swear by putting the things down to find some peace. Former Upwork CEO **Fabio Rosati** encouraged founders to put down their smartphones and show their loved ones respect—even when calls and emails are tugging at your sleeve.

"I would say that your entrepreneurial adventure could consume you, and it is imperative that you learn how to make sure that doesn't happen. You've got to have the tools to tame the beast, to take breaks, and most of all, to be present. It's so easy to be with your family or friends on holiday, and not be there, because you're really constantly being dragged back into work. I think that's a huge mistake. Be very aware to not sleep with your iPhone next to your bed or have your iPad next to your breakfast table, or not to be on email while your significant other is talking to you. Be there. Be present when you're home."

ONE HABIT THAT
I VALUE HIGHLY
IS TAKING A
NIGHTLY WALK
BEFORE BED TO
DISENGAGE, THINK
ABOUT THE DAY,
AND PREPARE
FOR SLEEP.

Joel Gascoigne
Co-founder & CEO, Buffer

Z

Z

Z

Z

Z

Arianna Huffington on Taking Care of Yourself

The media titan offered Foundr three great tips guaranteed to make your life more productive and fulfilling:

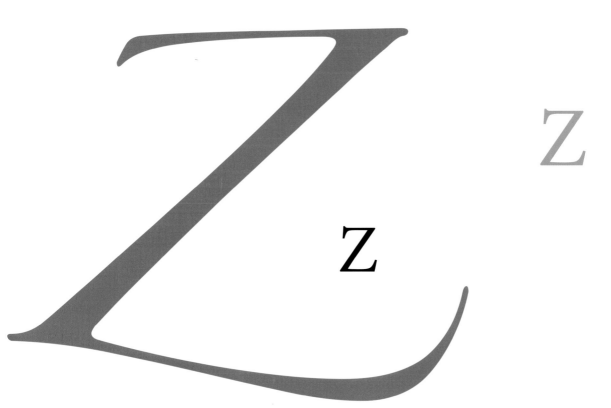

Sleep More

Wise people get enough sleep. As little as 30 minutes extra sleep every night is enough to transform your quality of life markedly. We tend to value being exhausted and overworked as badges of honor, but ultimately burning yourself out is an inherently unhealthy practice. If you can't sleep at night, embrace the idea of naps during the day.

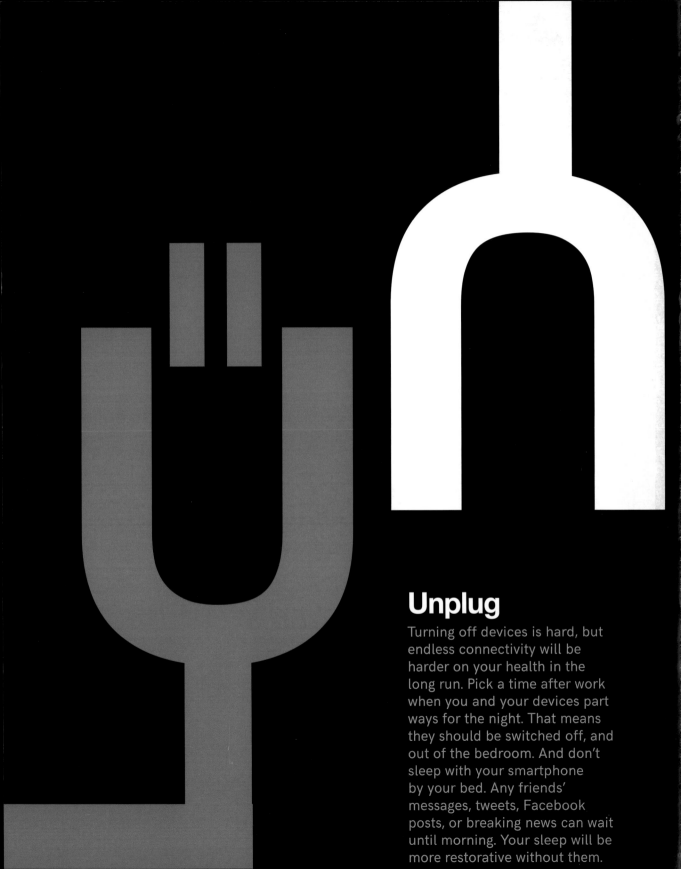

Unplug

Turning off devices is hard, but endless connectivity will be harder on your health in the long run. Pick a time after work when you and your devices part ways for the night. That means they should be switched off, and out of the bedroom. And don't sleep with your smartphone by your bed. Any friends' messages, tweets, Facebook posts, or breaking news can wait until morning. Your sleep will be more restorative without them.